ONE WITH THE FORCE

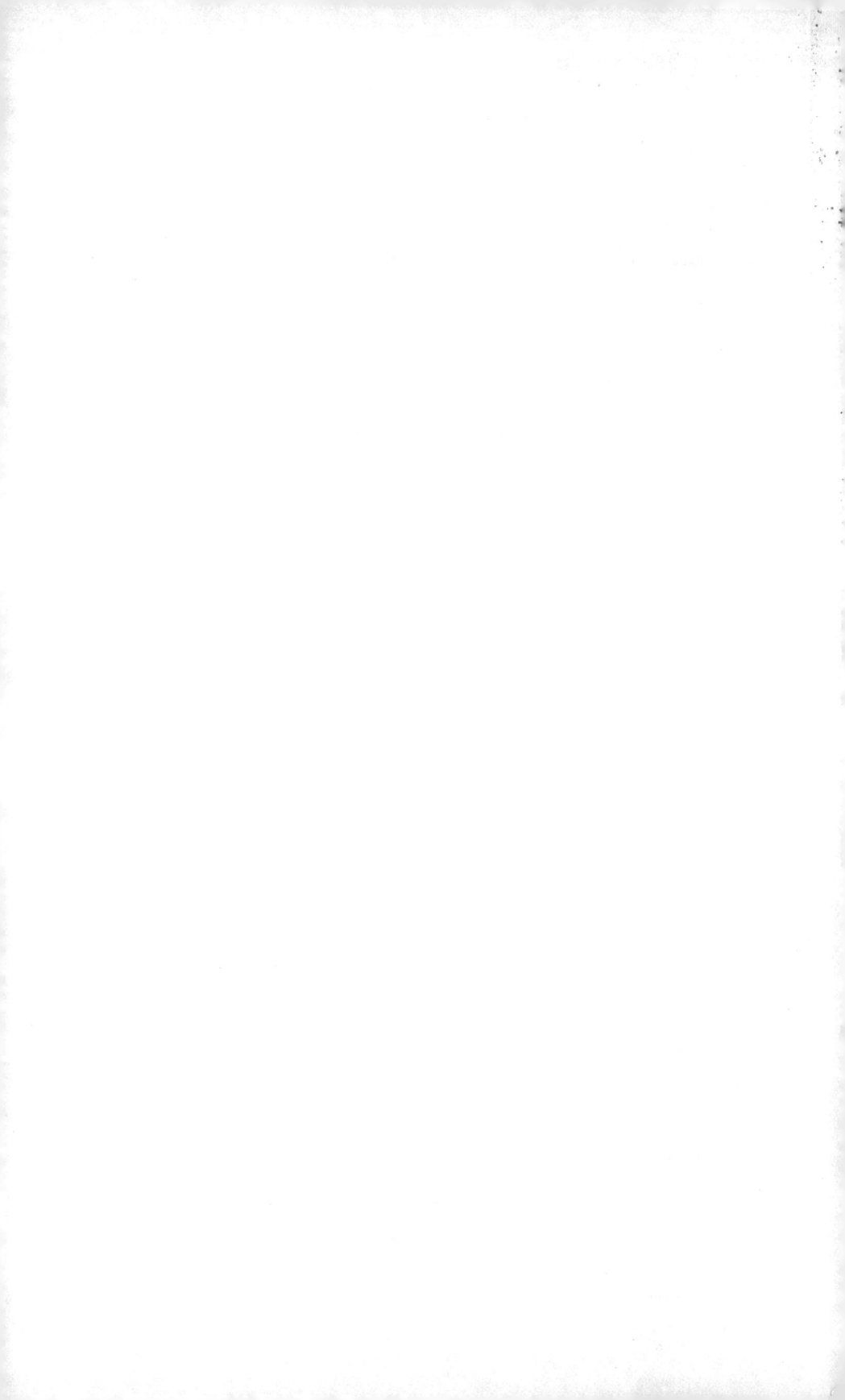

ONE WITH THE FORCE

18 Universal Truths in *Star Wars*

KRISTA NOBLE

ROWMAN & LITTLEFIELD
Lanham • Boulder • New York • London

Published by Rowman & Littlefield
An imprint of The Rowman & Littlefield Publishing Group, Inc.
4501 Forbes Boulevard, Suite 200, Lanham, Maryland 20706
www.rowman.com

86-90 Paul Street, London EC2A 4NE

British Library Cataloguing in Publication Information Available

Library of Congress Cataloging-in-Publication Data

Names: Noble, Krista, 1990– author.
Title: One with the force : 18 universal truths in Star Wars / Krista Noble.
Description: Lanham : Rowman & Littlefield Publishing Group, 2024. | Includes
  bibliographical references and index. | Summary: "This book provides an intimate
  portrait of eighteen universal truths in Star Wars—principles that are 'true for all
  time, all places and all people.' Readers will see that the philosophy of the Jedi
  doesn't only apply 'in a galaxy far, far away'; it is also highly relevant to everyday
  living"— Provided by publisher.
Identifiers: LCCN 2024019709 (print) | LCCN 2024019710 (ebook) | ISBN
  9781538198711 (cloth) | ISBN 9781538198728 (epub)
Subjects: LCSH: Star Wars films—History and criticism. | Philosophy in motion
  pictures. | Jedi (Fictitious characters) | LCGFT: Film criticism.
Classification: LCC PN1995.9.S695 N63 2024 (print) | LCC PN1995.9.S695 (ebook)
  | DDC 791.43/75—dc23/eng/20240515
LC record available at https://lccn.loc.gov/2024019709
LC ebook record available at https://lccn.loc.gov/2024019710

♾™ The paper used in this publication meets the minimum requirements of American National Standard for Information Sciences—Permanence of Paper for Printed Library Materials, ANSI/NISO Z39.48-1992.

To my parents, my sister, and my brother-in-law,
for their unwavering love and support

CONTENTS

ACKNOWLEDGMENTS

First, I would like to thank my parents, Paul and Michelle Noble; my sister, Alexi Noble; and my brother-in-law, Marco Panama, for their unwavering love and support. A special thanks goes to my dad, who introduced me to Vedic knowledge and gave me invaluable suggestions for enhancing this book.

Second, I want to thank my literary agent, Dawn Frederick; my editors, Deni Remsberg and Patricia Stevenson; my cover designer, Kathi Ha; and everyone at Rowman & Littlefield who helped prepare my manuscript for publication. Dawn's wise input greatly strengthened my book proposal, and Deni and Patricia were wonderful guides throughout the editorial process.

Third, I am thankful for the family members, friends, colleagues, and students who agreed to review this book. I truly appreciate their support.

Finally, I am grateful to my former professors at Maharishi International University for deepening my understanding and love of Vedic knowledge.

Part I

THE WISDOM OF THE EAST IN *STAR WARS*

Chapter 1

SETTING THE SCENE

There is no denying the phenomenal success of *Star Wars*. It is the second-highest-grossing movie franchise of all time, having earned over $10 billion at the worldwide box office.[1] It holds the Guinness World Record for "most successful film merchandising franchise."[2] It has spawned numerous creative works, from the hit television series *The Mandalorian* to a variety of popular video games and novels. It has even inspired attractions at Disney parks around the world.

For further evidence of the immense popularity of *Star Wars*, consider this: When the second trailer for *The Force Awakens* was released, more than thirty million people watched this video. As a result, it broke the Guinness World Record for "most viewed movie trailer on YouTube in 24 hours."[3]

Why do people love *Star Wars* so much? The answer to this question is multifaceted. It must consider factors such as George Lucas's imaginative world-building, John Williams's award-winning soundtracks, the films' groundbreaking special effects, and the appeal of actors like Harrison Ford, Carrie Fisher, and Mark Hamill. Other key factors include the concepts of the Force (an all-pervasive energy field) and the Jedi (warriors who use this field to achieve supernatural feats).

If you are a *Star Wars* fan, then you are already familiar with these concepts. You've watched Luke Skywalker destroy the Death Star in *A New Hope*. You've seen Yoda merge with the Force in *Return of the Jedi*. You've heard Rey contact the Jedi of the past in *The Rise of Skywalker*.

But did you know that the *Star Wars* films contain parallels to religions and philosophies from around the world—from Christianity to Buddhism, and from Native American teachings to the Vedic knowledge of ancient India?

This book will explore these parallels. Part I will discuss the profound similarities between the philosophy of *Star Wars* and Vedic knowledge. It will compare the Force to *Brahman*, meaning the consciousness that underlies and pervades the universe. It will connect the light and dark sides of the Force to *sattva* and *tamas*, the forces of creation and destruction. Part I will also relate the Jedi to the ancient *siddhas*, practitioners of yoga and meditation who allegedly obtained supernatural abilities. Along the way, it will delve into a rich array of topics, from the purpose of life to collective consciousness, and from enlightenment to immortality.

Part II will have a broader focus. It will examine *Star Wars* in relation to (1) the Eastern traditions of Buddhism, Taoism, and Sikhism; (2) the Western religions of Judaism, Christianity, and Islam; and (3) the teachings of various Native American and First Nations cultures. It will suggest that *Star Wars* contains eighteen universal truths—principles that are "true for all time, all places and all people."[4]

Let's begin our journey with the following question: Where did the concept of the Force come from?

WHERE DID THE FORCE COME FROM?

Intriguingly, the early drafts of the original *Star Wars* screenplay did not refer to "the Force," but rather "the force of others."[5] The first draft included the statement "May the Force of others be with you," but it did not explain this phrase. The salutation seemed to be a generic wish for good luck; most commentators agree that it was probably inspired by the Christian saying "May the Lord be with you." The second draft portrayed "the force of others" as a supernatural power, the source of the characters' miraculous abilities; it also introduced a "Kiber crystal," which enhanced these abilities. These basic concepts remained in the third draft.[6] It was not until the fourth draft that screenwriter George Lucas (born in 1944) shortened "the force of others" to "the Force" and removed references to the Kiber crystal.[7]

According to Michael Kaminski, author of *The Secret History of Star Wars*, Lucas found inspiration for "the force of others" in "comic books and science fiction novels . . . from Kirkby's *New Gods* saga to Smith's *Lensmen* saga."[8] The filmmaker was also inspired by the abstract movie *21-87* (released in 1963), which mentions a "force" that people refer to as "God."[9]

In addition, Lucas was influenced by Eastern philosophical traditions, many of which refer to an all-permeating "life-energy" or "life-force" (called *prana* in ancient Indian texts and *qi* or *chi* in traditional Chinese culture).[10]

Lucas was exposed to these Eastern traditions in part by Gary Kurtz (1940–2018), the producer of the first two *Star Wars* films.[11] Kurtz had a background in comparative religion, as well as in Buddhism, Hinduism, and Native American teachings. He discussed these topics at length with Lucas, recommending philosophical changes to the early drafts of the first *Star Wars* screenplay.

Lucas also encountered Eastern principles when he lived in the San Francisco Bay Area in the 1970s. This region was pervaded by New Age spirituality, which drew heavily on Eastern philosophy. The filmmaker wrote and directed the first *Star Wars* film during this time.

Furthermore, Lucas gained exposure to Eastern thought when he learned the Transcendental Meditation[12] technique and the Vedic (ancient Indian) concepts behind it. He began practicing this technique in the late 1960s[13] after the monk Maharishi Mahesh Yogi (1918–2008) introduced it to the West.[14] It is rumored that Lucas based the character of Yoda on Maharishi.[15]

The filmmaker has acknowledged the influence of Eastern traditions on *Star Wars*. He once said, "The 'Force of others' is what all basic religions are based on, *especially the Eastern religions*, which is, essentially, that there is a force, God, whatever you want to call it."[16] This statement provides a strong foundation for part II of this book, as it supports a connection between the Force and the Vedic principle of *Brahman* (the consciousness that underlies and pervades the universe).

Although the filmmaker drew inspiration from Eastern traditions, he had a universal perspective in mind when he created *Star Wars*. This point is clear from the following quote by Lucas:

> The Force evolved out of various developments of character and plot. I wanted a concept of religion based on the premise that there is a God and there is good and evil. I began to distill the essence of all religions into what I thought was a basic idea common to all religions and common to primitive thinking. I wanted to develop something that was nondenominational but still had a kind of religious reality. I believe in God and I believe in right and wrong. I also believe that there are basic tenets which through history have developed into certainties, such as "thou shalt not kill." I don't want to hurt other people. "Do unto others . . ." is the philosophy that permeates my work.[17]

Thus, the Force was based on Lucas's attempt to "distill the essence of all religions" into a single, core principle. He associates this "essence" with (1) a belief in God and (2) a belief in right and wrong. It makes sense that Lucas holds this view, given that the Force is like an abstract, all-pervading God, and the light and dark sides of the Force correspond to good and evil. Lucas also correlates "the essence of all religions" with treating others well and avoiding unnecessary violence—themes that are found in a variety of religious/philosophical traditions (see part II).

Lucas provides additional evidence of the universal perspective behind *Star Wars*: "I put the Force into the movies in order to try to awaken a certain kind of spirituality in young people."[18] The filmmaker's general reference to "spirituality" suggests that he was not endorsing any particular religion or philosophy.

As for Lucas's personal views, he has described himself as a "Methodist Buddhist."[19] This unusual combination of Western and Eastern beliefs again reveals a universal perspective on life.

Lucas developed this perspective in part due to the works of comparative mythologist Joseph Campbell (1904–1987).[20] Campbell wrote *The Hero with a Thousand Faces*, which highlights parallels between the mythologies of different cultures. Lucas was so inspired by this book that he modified a draft of the original *Star Wars* screenplay to better reflect Campbell's statements.[21] Eventually, Lucas and Campbell met and became friends.[22]

Thus, according to many sources (including Lucas himself), the *Star Wars* films were strongly influenced by Eastern philosophical traditions. Therefore, it makes sense to explore these movies in light of Eastern principles, including Vedic (ancient Indian) principles.

INTRODUCING THE VEDIC TRADITION: "DEEP, ORIGINAL, AND SUBLIME"

The Vedic tradition stems from the Vedas, a collection of ancient Indian texts.[23] According to orthodox teachings, the Vedas are essentially eternal and uncreated; they were cognized by seers during meditation. By contrast, according to Western scholars, these works were composed by human beings, passed down orally, and subsequently written down. Regardless of their exact origin, these Sanskrit texts include the Upanishads, which discuss yoga, meditation, enlightenment, and the nature of life. The Vedas gave rise to other notable works, such as the Yoga Sutra of Patanjali and the Bhagavad Gita.

Among the Vedic literature, the Upanishads have had an especially strong influence on Western thinkers. They have received praise from the following figures: American authors Ralph Waldo Emerson, Henry David Thoreau, and Walt Whitman; German philosophers Arthur Schopenhauer and Paul Deussen; and Nobel Prize–winning physicists Erwin Schrödinger and Niels Bohr.[24] Schopenhauer gave the following tribute to these ancient works:

> The Upanishads are the production of the highest human wisdom and I consider them almost superhuman in conception. The study of the Upanishads has been a source of great inspiration and means of comfort to my soul. From every sentence of the Upanishads deep, original and sublime thoughts arise, and the whole is pervaded by a high and holy and earnest spirit. In the whole world there is no study so beneficial and so elevating as that of the Upanishads. The Upanishads have been the solace of my life and will be the solace of my death.[25]

The Bhagavad Gita has also received accolades from famous individuals, including Swiss psychiatrist Carl Jung, German author Hermann Hesse, English author Aldous Huxley, American physicist J. Robert Oppenheimer, American authors Henry David Thoreau and Ralph Waldo Emerson, and Indian social activist Mohandas Gandhi.[26] Gandhi spoke of this work in glowing terms:

> I find a solace in the Bhagavad-Gita, in the Upanishads, that I miss even in the Sermon on the Mount. . . . When doubt haunts me, when disappointment stares me in the face and all alone I see not one ray of light, I go back to the Bhagavad-Gita. I find a verse here and a verse there and I immediately begin to smile in the midst of overwhelming sorrow, in the midst of overwhelming tragedies—and my life has been full of external tragedies—and if they have left no visible or no indelible scar upon me, I owe it all to the teachings of the Bhagavad-Gita.[27]

Clearly, these Vedic texts—the Upanishads and the Bhagavad Gita—deeply inspired the great thinkers mentioned earlier. Their enduring influence may be partially due to their universal perspective on life. From a Vedic standpoint, certain fundamental principles are *nitya*, meaning "true for all time, all places and all people."[28] The oldest of the Vedas, the Rig-Veda, expresses this idea: "Reality is one; the wise speak of it in different ways."[29] In other words, although human descriptions vary, the fundamental reality of life remains the same in all contexts.

These teachings correspond with George Lucas's desire to "distill the essence of all religions" into a single, core principle.[30] This universal perspective may be the ultimate reason *Star Wars* is so popular. These films resonate with people on a profound level—a level beyond superficial cultural, religious, and philosophical differences (see part II).

Before delving into these topics, you will want to be familiar with the main *Star Wars* films, which are briefly summarized below.

STAR WARS: PLOT SUMMARIES

If you're a *Star Wars* buff with detailed knowledge of the nine films in the Skywalker saga, then feel free to skip ahead to chapter 2. But if you're new to this franchise or want to refresh your memory of the films, this section is for you. The following summaries focus on the journeys of the main characters: Luke Skywalker, Anakin Skywalker, and Rey.

The Original Trilogy

The original trilogy stars Mark Hamill, Harrison Ford, and Carrie Fisher and includes the following films: *A New Hope* (1977; originally titled *Star Wars*),[31] *The Empire Strikes Back* (1980),[32] and *Return of the Jedi* (1983).[33]

Like all the *Star Wars* films, the original trilogy is set in a distant galaxy. It depicts a period of civil war between the tyrannical Galactic Empire and the Rebel Alliance. The hero of this trilogy is Luke Skywalker, who begins as a humble nineteen-year-old farm boy living on the desert planet of Tatooine.

In *A New Hope*, Luke encounters Obi-Wan "Ben" Kenobi, an old Jedi Master (the Jedi are warriors who strive to maintain peace and justice in the galaxy). Luke agrees to travel with Obi-Wan to assist Princess Leia Organa, a young member of the Rebellion. Four other characters join the expedition: Han Solo, a charming smuggler; Chewbacca, a large, furry creature called a Wookie; and C-3PO and R2-D2, two helpful droids. Along the way, Obi-Wan teaches Luke how to use the Force, an all-pervading energy field, to achieve supernatural feats. The boy and his companions rescue Princess Leia; however, Obi-Wan is killed by Darth Vader, a former Jedi who turned to "the dark side of the Force." Vader is now a Sith Lord, a warrior who uses the Force to increase his power. In the film's climax, Luke joins the Rebels and uses the Force to destroy the Death Star, the battle station and supreme weapon of the Empire.

In *The Empire Strikes Back*, a small creature named Yoda teaches Luke the ways of the Jedi. But Luke leaves his training when he realizes that his friends Han and Leia are in danger. In his attempt to rescue them, Luke comes face to face with Darth Vader. The two duel with lightsabers, the traditional weapons of the Jedi and the Sith. During this confrontation, Luke is shocked to learn that Vader is his father. The young man loses the fight, but he and his friends manage to escape—except for Han, who has been frozen in carbonite and given to a bounty hunter.

In *Return of the Jedi*, Luke and his companions rescue Han from the nefarious gangster Jabba the Hutt. Luke also visits Yoda, who dies of old age. Shortly thereafter, Luke encounters the spirit of Obi-Wan and learns that Leia is his twin sister. Finally, the young man faces Darth Vader for the second time; he defeats his father in battle but refuses to kill him. The evil Emperor Palpatine tortures Luke, but Vader intervenes; he destroys the emperor and saves his son's life. Through these actions, Vader returns to "the light side of the Force." He reconciles with Luke before dying of his wounds. Meanwhile, the Rebel forces launch their final attack against the Empire and win the war. In the last scene, Luke, now a full-fledged Jedi Knight, watches the Rebels' celebration with his friends. The spirits of Obi-Wan, Yoda, and Anakin Skywalker (Vader's true name) observe from the shadows, smiling.

The Prequel Trilogy

The prequel trilogy features Liam Neeson, Ewan McGregor, Natalie Portman, Jake Lloyd, and Hayden Christensen and includes the following films: *The Phantom Menace* (1999),[34] *Attack of the Clones* (2002),[35] and *Revenge of the Sith* (2005).[36]

The events of this trilogy precede the events of the original movies. The prequel trilogy is set in the days of the Old Republic, before the existence of the Galactic Empire. It chronicles the downfall of Luke's father, Anakin Skywalker. As mentioned earlier, Anakin was a Jedi who turned to the dark side of the Force and became Darth Vader.

In *The Phantom Menace*, Anakin (nicknamed "Ani") seems anything but sinister; he is just a nine-year-old slave boy who is strong with the Force. Qui-Gon Jinn, a Jedi Master, discovers the boy's abilities. He thinks that Anakin is the "Chosen One" prophesied to restore the balance between the light and dark sides of the Force. Qui-Gon wishes to train the boy to become a Jedi, even though the Jedi Council disapproves. Unfortunately, Qui-Gon is fatally wounded by a Sith Lord named Darth Maul. In his final moments, the Jedi Master asks his apprentice, the young Obi-Wan, to train Anakin.

In *Attack of the Clones*, Anakin is Obi-Wan's nineteen-year-old apprentice. The teenager falls in love with the beautiful Senator Padmé Amidala, whom he has been assigned to protect from a Separatist movement. Sadly, Anakin and Padmé's love is forbidden since the Jedi Code prohibits romantic relationships. Anakin journeys to his home planet, Tatooine, with Padmé and discovers that his mother has been mortally injured by Tusken Raiders. Enraged, he slaughters the Tusken tribe. Next, Anakin and Padmé travel to the planet of Geonosis to help Obi-Wan, who has been imprisoned by the Separatist movement. The mission fails; the two lovers are captured and sentenced to death, as is Obi-Wan. However, leading an army of clones, Yoda and the other Jedi rescue the trio. At the end of the film, Anakin marries Padmé in secret.

In *Revenge of the Sith*, Padmé becomes pregnant, and Anakin has visions of her dying in childbirth. This situation plays into the hands of Supreme Chancellor Palpatine, who is plotting to become the Galactic Emperor. Palpatine, secretly known as Darth Sidious, claims that the Sith possess the knowledge of how to prevent death. Desperate for this knowledge, Anakin turns to the dark side of the Force. He accepts the title "Darth Vader" and takes part in Palpatine's quest to eradicate the Jedi. In a moment of anger, Vader even hurts Padmé. Obi-Wan intervenes; he duels with his former apprentice, gravely injures him, and sorrowfully leaves him for dead. Palpatine rescues Vader, who receives a black, armored suit and a mask that helps him breathe. Elsewhere, Padmé gives birth to twins—namely, Luke and Leia—before she dies. The twins are sent to other planets to keep them safe, and Obi-Wan and Yoda go into exile.

The Sequel Trilogy

The sequel trilogy stars Daisy Ridley, Adam Driver, John Boyega, and Oscar Isaac, as well as the main actors from the original trilogy (Mark Hamill, Harrison Ford, and Carrie Fisher), and includes the following films: *The Force Awakens* (2015),[37] *The Last Jedi* (2017),[38] and *The Rise of Skywalker* (2019).[39]

The events of the sequel trilogy take place thirty years after the events of the original trilogy. In this latest trilogy, a new threat has arisen: the oppressive First Order, which aims to destroy the New Republic. To counteract this dictatorship, General Leia Organa (formerly known as Princess

Leia) leads a Resistance movement. But the hero of the story is Rey, a nineteen-year-old orphan girl who is strong in the Force.

In *The Force Awakens*, Rey encounters BB-8, a droid who has a map of Luke Skywalker's secret location. She also meets Finn, a former First Order stormtrooper (a type of elite soldier). When the First Order launches an airstrike on Rey's home planet (Jakku), she, Finn, and BB-8 flee in the *Millennium Falcon* (Han Solo's starship). Soon, Han and Chewbacca board the ship. Together, Rey, Finn, Han, and Chewbacca plan to deliver BB-8 to the Resistance. But when they visit the planet Takodana, Kylo Ren, a First Order commander, captures Rey. Kylo (previously known as Ben Solo) is Han and Leia's son, a former Jedi apprentice who turned to the dark side of the Force. He takes Rey to Starkiller Base, a planet transformed into a powerful weapon, where he interrogates her. However, Rey resists Kylo's attempts to read her mind and escapes using the Force. Meanwhile, the Resistance fighters plan to destroy Starkiller Base. Han, Chewbacca, Finn, and (later) Rey take part in this mission, as does Poe Dameron, a courageous pilot and BB-8's owner. The operation is successful, but before the base implodes, Kylo Ren kills his father, Han Solo. The young commander also duels with Rey, who defeats him; the two are separated when Starkiller Base begins to self-destruct. Rey, Finn, Chewbacca, and Poe return safely to the Resistance. In the final scene, Rey finds Luke, who has been living in exile on the oceanic planet of Ahch-To.

In *The Last Jedi*, Luke, now a Jedi Master, reluctantly teaches Rey to use the Force. Around this time, the young woman discovers that her mind is linked to Kylo's; she can communicate with the First Order commander across great distances. Rey senses that Kylo is conflicted and journeys to meet him, hoping to bring him back to the light side of the Force. Unfortunately, Kylo imprisons her and presents her to his master, Supreme Leader Snoke. Snoke tortures Rey, wanting to discover Luke's whereabouts, and then orders Kylo to kill her; however, the young commander kills the supreme leader instead. Kylo and Rey fight Snoke's guards side by side and defeat them. Kylo then asks Rey to join him and rule together, but she refuses and escapes the starship. They encounter each other again on the planet of Crait, where Kylo—now the supreme leader—commands the First Order to attack the Resistance base. Luke distracts the First Order by projecting an image of himself from far away, thereby buying time for the rebels to evacuate. Rey also helps, using the Force to remove a rocky barrier blocking the escape route. Thanks to Luke and Rey's efforts, the Resistance survives (though Luke dies from the effort of maintaining his illusion).

In *The Rise of Skywalker*, the Resistance hears that Emperor Palpatine has risen from the dead and built a secret armada called the Final Order. Rey, Finn, Poe, Chewbacca, BB-8, and C-3PO search for a Sith Wayfinder, a device that will lead them to the emperor's location. Along the way, Rey learns that she is Palpatine's granddaughter. She also encounters Kylo Ren and duels with him again. In the middle of the fight, Kylo's mother, Leia, reaches out to her son through the Force; she whispers his true name, Ben, and dies. This contact distracts Kylo, allowing Rey to impale him; however, she then uses the Force to heal him. In the wake of these events, Kylo decides to return to the light side of the Force. Rey uses Kylo/Ben's Wayfinder to locate Palpatine, transmitting her coordinates to the Resistance. She confronts the sinister emperor on the planet of Exegol. Palpatine reveals that he wants Rey to kill him so that the spirits of the Sith can pass into her. Rey refuses to comply; instead, she gives her lightsaber to Ben, who has arrived to help her. Palpatine drains Ben and Rey's power and attacks the Resistance fleet. Rey collapses, but the Jedi of the past speak to her and bolster her strength. She rises to confront Palpatine, who tries to strike her with Force lightning. Rey blocks the attack, causing the emperor's lightning to rebound and destroy him. She is fatally wounded, but Ben uses the Force to heal her, which costs him his life. They kiss, and he dies. Above, the Resistance defeats the Final Order. In the last scene, Rey buries Luke's and Leia's lightsabers on Tatooine, where Luke grew up. She sees their spirits watching her and decides to adopt their family name: Skywalker.

Now that you're familiar with the characters and events of the main *Star Wars* films, let's turn to the parallels between *Star Wars* and the Vedic tradition, beginning with the similarities between the Force and *Brahman*.

Chapter 2

THE FORCE AND UNIVERSAL CONSCIOUSNESS (*BRAHMAN*)

"May the Force be with you." This phrase, which appears in *A New Hope* and multiple other *Star Wars* films, is one of the most iconic lines in cinematic history.[1] It ranks number 8 on the American Film Institute's list of the "100 Greatest Movie Quotes of All Time" and number 4 on *The Hollywood Reporter*'s list of "Hollywood's 100 Favorite Movie Quotes."[2] This phrase has permeated popular culture, from T-shirts to online memes to references in television shows and movies.[3] It has even inspired an informal *Star Wars* holiday, May 4. "*May the 4th* be with you" is a play on "May the Force be with you."[4]

But what exactly is "the Force"? In the *Star Wars* films, the Jedi Masters address this question in different ways. Luke Skywalker gives an intriguing explanation in *The Last Jedi*: "[The Force is] the energy between all things, a tension, a balance, that binds the universe together."[5]

There are many parallels between the Force and the Vedic principle of *Brahman*, meaning the consciousness that underlies and pervades the universe.

PARALLELS

According to the Upanishads, a famous collection of Vedic texts, a universal level of consciousness is the basis of individual consciousness. This cosmic awareness is the source of the orderly intelligence of all creatures. It is like an ocean, whereas particular minds are like waves on the surface; the ocean connects the waves, unifying them at their foundation. This "ocean," sometimes called "pure consciousness," is characterized by infinite energy and creativity.

To address the relationship between pure consciousness and the physical world, let's borrow an analogy from the Chandogya Upanishad.[6] Suppose that you add salt to a bowl of water and leave it overnight. The following morning, you take a sip from the center of the bowl. How does it taste? Salty, of course. Next, you take sips from the right and left sides of the bowl; you find that these areas are also salty. You realize that it doesn't matter which part you sample because the salt permeates every drop.

As the Chandogya Upanishad explains, the same goes for pure consciousness: It permeates every object in the physical world. Indeed, it is the source and essence of all things. It is beyond the physical senses; it cannot be seen, heard, touched, smelled, or tasted. The Mundaka Upanishad describes this level of reality as follows:

> That which is beyond sight, beyond grasp, without source,
> without features, without eyes or ears, without hands or feet,
> eternal, all-pervading, omnipresent, extremely subtle—that is
> the imperishable, which the wise know as the womb of beings.[7]

The Vedic term for the imperishable, all-pervading pure consciousness is *Brahman*. Recall Luke's statement from the beginning of this chapter: "[The Force is] the energy between all things, a tension, a balance, that binds the universe together."[8] Based on this quote and various *Star Wars* scenes, here are three similarities between the Force and *Brahman*:

1. Both are associated with energy. The Force is "the energy between all things," and *Brahman* contains infinite energy, through which it sustains the world.
2. Both are all-pervading. The Force "binds the universe together," which suggests that it is omnipresent. Likewise, *Brahman* is in all places, like the salt permeating every drop of water.
3. Both are beyond the reach of the physical senses; it is impossible to detect the Force or *Brahman* using our normal organs of perception (eyes, ears, hands, and so on).

Although Luke does not say that the Force is beyond the physical senses, various scenes in *Star Wars* illustrate this idea.

THE FORCE: BEYOND THE PHYSICAL SENSES

In *Star Wars*, one cannot perceive the Force through sight, scent, taste, touch, or smell. Indeed, to feel and use this energy field, it is helpful to transcend the physical senses.

These are important themes in *A New Hope*. For example, consider the scene in which young Luke learns to wield a lightsaber. He struggles to use this weapon to block laser beams emitted by a hovering robot. Obi-Wan Kenobi then places a helmet over the boy's head that obstructs his vision. The Jedi Master cautions Luke not to trust his eyes, as they may deceive him. In other words, the boy should stop relying on his physical senses.

Instead, Obi-Wan tells Luke to do the following: (1) "Let go your conscious self." (2) "Act on instinct." (3) "Stretch out with your feelings."[9] By heeding this advice, Luke connects with and uses the all-pervading Force to his advantage. He gains a subtle awareness of the robot's movements and succeeds in blocking the laser beams.

The theme of going beyond the senses reaches its culmination at the end of *A New Hope*. At this point, the Rebel Alliance is attacking the Death Star, the battle station and supreme weapon of the evil Empire. Luke, flying one of the Rebel starships, is trying to fire on a small weak spot on the Death Star. At first, he relies on his computerized targeting system to navigate, until Obi-Wan's disembodied voice says, "Use the Force, Luke."[10] After some hesitation, the boy turns off the system, thereby diminishing his reliance on his physical senses. This decision allows him to connect with the Force, giving him an intuitive sense of the perfect moment to release his torpedo. Luke fires, setting off a chain reaction that destroys the Death Star. Afterward, he pauses with his eyes closed, keeping his senses disengaged for a moment longer.

In summary, both of these scenes highlight the value of transcending the senses in order to feel and use the Force. Similar themes are found in the Vedic tradition.

BRAHMAN: BEYOND THE PHYSICAL SENSES

To understand the similarities just mentioned, one needs to be familiar with a few Vedic principles. For instance, according to Vedic teachings, it is possible to experience unity with pure consciousness. After all, this cosmic awareness is the basis of individual awareness; it is the fundamental Self of all beings. So, it's simply a matter of teaching the mind to realize its essential nature. It's like causing a wave to settle down so that it merges with the ocean.

Still, there are obstacles to this experience of unity. For instance, there are the five senses, which ordinarily keep the mind engrossed in the superficial, physical level of life. As the Bhagavad Gita states, "When a man's mind is governed by any of the wandering senses, his intellect is carried away by it as a ship by the wind on water."[11] In other words, the senses absorb one's attention; as a result, they obscure the transcendental reality of pure consciousness. Therefore, to experience union with the Self, one must slip beyond all perceptions, as well as thoughts and emotions.

This experience of union is called "yoga." Although in the West this term is associated with physical exercises, it also refers to a distinct state of consciousness. To quote the Yoga Sutra of Patanjali, an ancient Indian text, "Yoga is the complete settling of the activity of the mind."[12] In other words, one reaches the state of yoga when all mental activity has faded away and yet one is still awake. This state is typically reached during meditation, though it can come at other times as well.

One may wonder what it is like to be awake without the fears and frustrations that often clutter our minds—to be aware without any particular object of awareness. The Tejobindu Upanishad describes this state with the phrase *sat chit ananda*, which means "eternal bliss consciousness."[13] The first word, "eternal" (*sat*), is related to the experience of timelessness in the state of yoga. In this state, the meditator has completely lost awareness of time, space, and other limiting factors. The next word, "bliss" (*ananda*), means the deep, unwavering joy that characterizes this state. Unlike everyday happiness, this joy does not depend on anything in the external world; it exists within. To quote the Vedic teacher Ravi Shankar (born in 1956), "I tell you, deep inside you is a fountain of bliss, a fountain of joy. Deep inside your center core is truth, light, love, there is no guilt there, there is no fear there. . . . Psychologists have never looked deep enough."[14] The last word, "consciousness" (*chit*), reveals that in the state of yoga, the meditator is awake—not asleep or unconscious.

From a Vedic perspective, in the state of yoga, you are awake to your own consciousness, your own nature, your own essential Self—nothing more.[15] You experience who you are on the most fundamental level, beyond all stresses and distractions. And "who you are" is eternal bliss consciousness: infinite, immortal, and joyful. (Note that "eternal bliss consciousness" is synonymous with "pure consciousness"; these two phrases simply highlight different aspects of the same cosmic awareness.)

In the Upanishads, yoga is referred to as the fourth state of consciousness (or simply "the fourth"). It is beyond the three basic states of waking,
dreaming, and deep sleep. The Nrisimhottaratapaniya Upanishad describes
"the fourth" as follows: "The peaceful, the blissful, the undivided is thought
to be the fourth; that is the Self. That is to be known."[16] In other words,
the state of yoga is peaceful and blissful; it is also undivided, meaning that it
involves union with the Self. "That is to be known" encourages the reader
to experience this state of awareness firsthand.

It is important to note that the state of yoga cannot be forced. It cannot be reached by trying to feel blissful or focusing on the concept of *sat
chit ananda*. Such attempts will keep you on the level of the emotions or
intellect; the point is to get beyond these levels—to enjoy "the complete
settling of the activity of the mind."[17] Fortunately, the state of yoga can be
achieved naturally and spontaneously through certain traditional styles of
meditation.[18]

The existence of this state has been verified by multiple peer-reviewed
scientific studies. In one of these studies, the researchers arrived at the
following conclusions: "Subjectively, this state [of yoga, or Transcendental
Consciousness][19] is characterized by the absence of the very framework
(time, space, and body sense) and content (qualities of inner and outer
perception) that define waking experiences."[20] Thus, in the state of yoga,
the meditator has transcended awareness of time, space, body sense, and
perceptual content.

This state of awareness can also be described in objective terms since
it has distinct neurophysiological markers: "slow inhalation, along with
autonomic orientation at the onset of breath changes and heightened $\alpha 1$
[alpha 1] (8–10 Hz) frontal coherence."[21] These physical patterns reveal a
state of "restful alertness."[22] (For scientific studies about the state of yoga,
see appendix B.)

The transcendental experience doesn't completely vanish after meditation; it lingers to some degree after each session. Through regular practice,
the deep peace of eternal bliss consciousness begins to coexist with our
thoughts and actions. Eventually, this state of awareness can become permanent, unshaken by anything that happens in the world. That is the true
goal of yogic practice. To quote the Yoga Sutra again, "Yoga becomes firmly
established through regular and respectful practice for a long time."[23] The
permanent state of yoga is sometimes referred to as "Cosmic Consciousness"
or "enlightenment."[24]

Several peer-reviewed scientific studies support the existence of this
state. Subjectively, it is "marked by inner self-awareness coexisting with

waking, sleeping, and dreaming."[25] Stated another way, the individual never loses awareness of the Self, even during sleep. Physiologically, the permanent state of yoga "is marked by the coexistence of α1 [alpha 1] electroencephalography (EEG) with delta EEG during deep sleep."[26] In other words, alpha 1 brainwaves, which are associated with "transcendental experiences during meditation,"[27] are seen alongside delta brainwaves, which are the normal indicators of deep sleep. The permanent state of yoga also correlates with "higher brain integration, greater emotional stability, and decreased anxiety during challenging tasks."[28] All these factors increase the individual's chances of success in life. (For scientific studies about the permanent state of yoga, see appendix B.)

Although this state is deeply fulfilling, it is not the highest state of human awareness. According to the Advaita Vedanta (nondualistic) school of thought, that designation belongs to *brahmi chetana*, which is sometimes referred to as "Unity Consciousness."[29] This exalted state of awareness develops naturally through continued meditation practice. In *brahmi chetana*, one spontaneously perceives that all things are the expressions of the same universal consciousness. This is like realizing that the waves are the expressions of the same underlying ocean. One is constantly aware of the transcendental unity underlying all diversity. One still sees distinctions between objects; however, one recognizes that these objects are part of a single, integrated wholeness. This wholeness is called *Brahman*.

In the philosophy of Advaita Vedanta, *brahmi chetana* is the pinnacle of human awareness; it is the purpose and goal of our existence. This state is described in the following excerpt from the Bhagavad Gita: "[He] sees the Self in all beings, and all beings in the Self."[30] In other words, the realized individual sees all beings as the expressions of the Self, pure consciousness.

From a Vedic standpoint, *brahmi chetana* cannot be attained through superficial intellectual exercises, such as repeatedly thinking, "I am one with the universe." Rather, this state of awareness depends on the purification of the body and mind, which typically requires years of regular meditation. Indeed, the states of yoga and *brahmi chetana* are not a matter of philosophy, attitude, or mood; instead, they are based on distinct styles of physiological functioning.[31] Because they are beyond the basic states of waking, dreaming, and deep sleep, they are referred to as "higher states of consciousness."

These states do not cause a permanent loss of individuality. On the surface, one remains a distinct person with specific traits and goals. One simply experiences that one is *more* than that—that, ultimately, one has a universal nature.

These Vedic principles are closely linked to *Star Wars*. In *A New Hope*, Luke must go beyond the physical senses to use the Force. Likewise, in the Vedic tradition, one must transcend the senses to experience the state of pure consciousness and enliven this state in one's life.

Both *Star Wars* and Vedic teachings (especially the Advaita Vedanta school of thought) support the following principles:

1. There is a reality beyond the sensory level of life. In other words, life is not restricted to the physical world that we can see, hear, smell, touch, and taste.
2. This transcendental reality is open to direct experience. In *Star Wars*, one can attain this experience by letting go of one's conscious self and reaching out with one's feelings (to paraphrase Obi-Wan's instructions in *A New Hope*). In the Vedic tradition, one can gain this experience through meditation, which allows the individual self to unite with the universal Self.

Now, in *Star Wars*, the Jedi do not merely feel the Force; they also use this energy field to achieve specific results. From a Vedic perspective, meditators may "use" pure consciousness in a similar way.

USING THE FORCE AND ENLIVENING COSMIC INTELLIGENCE

According to Vedic teachings, a person may "use" pure consciousness by enlivening cosmic intelligence within themselves, which will promote success in their endeavors. After all, pure consciousness (i.e., *Brahman*) is the source of the universe. It contains infinite intelligence, through which it governs the world in a positive, evolutionary direction.[32] When an individual unites with this universal awareness through meditation, they awaken its intelligence within themselves. Therefore, they spontaneously begin to think and act in a more orderly, creative, and progressive manner. Furthermore, the unbounded intelligence starts to support their actions, improving their rate of success.

Suppose that a person wishes to switch career paths. By meditating and enlivening cosmic intelligence, they will have a clearer sense of how to proceed. They will also increase the probability that the universe will facilitate their desire.

Thus, the Vedic tradition teaches that meditation can improve one's chances of achieving their goals. This could happen on a small scale; for instance, one might encounter lots of green lights on the way to an important appointment. Or it could occur on a larger scale; one might establish a thriving business or find their soulmate.

Enlivening universal intelligence through meditation is akin to using the Force, which also yields results on both small and large scales. On a small scale, a Jedi might detect the presence of another Force-sensitive individual. On a large scale, they might release the "one in a million" shot that destroys the Death Star, as Luke does in *A New Hope*.[33] Now that's some serious cosmic support!

This type of support is not a matter of luck. In *Star Wars*, it occurs when one uses the all-pervading Force to their advantage. In the Vedic tradition, it happens when one accesses a universal (and therefore more powerful) level of reality: pure consciousness.

These principles remind us of the *Star Wars* phrase "May the Force be with you." The Vedic version of this statement might run as follows: "May cosmic intelligence support you."

From a Vedic standpoint, it is possible for individuals to directly manifest a particular outcome. This result happens when a meditator (1) reaches the state of pure consciousness and (2) has an intention while in this state. For instance, they might have the intention of gaining greater happiness or knowledge. When this occurs, universal intelligence supports the meditator's goal. This concept recalls the Jedi, who regularly use the Force to achieve specific results.

The more spiritually evolved one is, the more likely they are to receive cosmic support in their endeavors. Thus, at any given time, some meditators may experience more support than others, depending on their current state of consciousness. An enlightened individual (one who has attained a permanent state of yoga) will typically be more successful at fulfilling their goals than the average person.

We find a similar concept in *Star Wars*. At any given time, some Jedi (and Sith) will be better at using the Force than others. For example, in *The Empire Strikes Back*, the Jedi Master Yoda is obviously more skilled at this than the young Luke. Consider the scene in which Luke attempts to lift his starship out of the swamp through the power of his mind; he fails to do so, whereas Yoda completes this task with ease. As the Jedi Master explains, the Force is his "ally," meaning that it supports his undertakings.[34] This statement does not yet fully apply to Luke; he must complete his training before he masters the traditional Jedi abilities.

These points relate to Yoda's famous line: "Try not. Do. Or do not. There is no try."[35] Because the Force is his ally, the Jedi Master does not need to try; all he needs to do is act, and his intention will be fulfilled.

This idea has parallels in the Vedic tradition, which teaches that enlightened individuals do not have to struggle. All they must do is act, and—in most cases—cosmic intelligence will support their goals.

In comparing Vedic principles with *Star Wars*, one should remember that the Force can be used for good or evil, whereas enlivening cosmic intelligence only increases evolutionary outcomes. This point represents a difference between the philosophy of *Star Wars* and Vedic teachings. However, the concept of the dark side of the Force *does* have parallels in the Vedic tradition—more on that topic in the next chapter.

We've seen that, from a Vedic perspective, meditators may experience greater success than the average person. However, that doesn't address whether they can perform Jedi feats like mind control or making objects float.

"SUPERNATURAL" ABILITIES: THE JEDI AND THE ANCIENT *SIDDHAS*

Few modern meditators would claim to have "supernatural" abilities. However, according to the Vedic tradition, ancient individuals called *siddhas* did attain such abilities, including knowledge of the future, levitation, mastery over the elements, and astral (out-of-body) travel.[36] Theoretically, these skills stemmed from gaining union with pure consciousness—the most fundamental level of life—and then acting from that level.

There are many parallels to these special abilities in the *Star Wars* films. As mentioned earlier, in *The Empire Strikes Back*, Yoda lifts Luke's starship out of the swamp using the power of his mind (demonstrating mastery over the elements). Later in the same film, Luke glimpses the future, seeing his friends trapped in a city among the clouds (demonstrating premonition). At the end of *The Last Jedi*, a much older Luke hovers in the air while projecting his awareness and image to another planet (demonstrating levitation and out-of-body travel). In each case, the Jedi accomplish their "supernatural" feats by connecting with and using the omnipresent Force.

In modern society, we apply the word "supernatural" to alleged events that seem inconsistent with the laws of nature. For instance, if someone were to levitate, we would consider this occurrence supernatural because it evidently contradicts the law of gravity.

However, suppose that the Force was real—an actual aspect of nature. In that case, using the Force would not be a supernatural act; one would simply be accessing and utilizing a different level of nature than usual. Let's also suppose that this level of reality was more fundamental, and therefore more powerful, than the sensory level (just as quantum physics is more fundamental and powerful than classical Newtonian physics). If so, then the Force might override more superficial forces, such as gravity. Thus, in the *Star Wars* universe, abilities like levitation might not be supernatural at all; rather, they might simply depend on accessing deeper levels of nature.

The same goes for Vedic teachings. If these teachings were true, then pure consciousness would be the basis of nature. So, if people learned to act from this level, even in extraordinary ways, then their actions would be profoundly natural, not supernatural.

In short, if one were to accept the worldview of the Jedi or the ancient *siddhas*, then one might need to expand their understanding of words like "nature" and "natural." With this broader understanding, they might not use the term "supernatural" in the same way as before.

MEDITATION AND YOGA POSTURES

In *Star Wars*, we occasionally see the Jedi meditating. This occurs several times in the prequel trilogy. For instance, in *The Phantom Menace*, Qui-Gon Jinn and Darth Maul are briefly separated in the middle of their duel; Qui-Gon uses this opportunity to meditate. Likewise, in *Attack of the Clones*, Anakin Skywalker meditates prior to a conversation with Padmé Amidala. In addition, in a deleted scene from *Revenge of the Sith*, Yoda is meditating when he hears the voice of the deceased Qui-Gon.[37] In each case, the Jedi meditate to connect with the Force.

This act is analogous to individuals in the Vedic tradition who meditate to connect with pure consciousness (i.e., the Self). The Self is always within them, whether they are aware of it or not. It is like the sun, which is always present, even when hidden behind clouds.

This concept has parallels in *Star Wars*. Consider the scene in *The Last Jedi* in which Luke teaches Rey about the Force. He asks her to share what she perceives in her surroundings. First, Rey mentions pairs of opposites, such as life and death, warmth and cold, and peace and violence. Next, she refers to the all-pervading Force. Last, she states, "Inside me the same Force."[38] Thus, Rey reveals that the Force is within the Jedi—just as, from a Vedic standpoint, the Self is within every human being.

In the scene described above, Luke tells Rey to sit cross-legged, close her eyes, and breathe. Here, he sounds like a yoga teacher. Indeed, yoga contains various cross-legged positions, such as *sukhasana* ("easy pose"), *siddhasana* ("accomplished pose"), and *padmasana* ("lotus pose"). It also includes breathing exercises, called *pranayama*. For a deeper experience, one may close their eyes during these practices.

In subsequent *Star Wars* scenes, we see the Jedi sit in traditional yoga postures. Consider the scene in *The Last Jedi* in which Luke projects his awareness and image to another planet; while doing so, he hovers in the air in *padmasana* ("lotus pose"). Also take the scene in *The Rise of Skywalker* in which Rey first tries to connect with the Jedi of the past; she is floating above the jungle floor in *sukhasana* ("easy pose"). Luke's and Rey's suspension in midair recalls the Yoga Sutra, which refers to the possibility of human levitation.

Like the Jedi, many meditators practice yoga. These postures have been part of the Vedic tradition since ancient times; they are mentioned in the Upanishads. The Jedi and Vedic meditators even hold similar views regarding the goal of yoga. From a Jedi perspective, the aim is to connect with the Force; from a Vedic standpoint, it is to connect with pure consciousness (i.e., the Self).

Chapter 3

LIGHT, DARKNESS,
SATTVA, AND *TAMAS*

Tension. This quality characterizes all the *Star Wars* films—the tension between good and evil, between light and darkness. The Jedi strive to embody the light side of the Force, while the Sith embrace the dark side. Certain characters, like Anakin Skywalker and Ben Solo, switch sides, falling into darkness and then rising again into the light.

As we will see, the Vedic tradition also contains the principles of spiritual light and darkness.

CREATION, DESTRUCTION, AND THE
TWO SIDES OF THE FORCE

As previously mentioned, in *The Last Jedi*, Luke Skywalker refers to the Force as "a tension . . . that binds the universe together."[1] Later in the same scene, he tells the young hero, Rey, to "reach out with [her] feelings" and share what she perceives.[2] In her response, Rey describes pairs of opposites: life and death, warmth and cold, and peace and violence. Luke asks what lies "between it all," to which Rey replies, "Balance. And energy. A Force."[3] This dialogue clarifies what Luke means by "tension"; apparently, he is referring to the tension between opposites, which the Force embodies.

These concepts have profound parallels in the Vedic tradition. Similar to the Force, pure consciousness is the basis of all opposites, including those just mentioned (life and death, peace and violence, and so on). We observe the tension between these diametric values in the world around us.

Incidentally, positive qualities like peace are closer to the essential nature of pure consciousness than negative ones like violence. As previously discussed, pure consciousness is intrinsically joyful; that's why it is called eternal bliss consciousness (*sat chit ananda*). And positive characteristics are more blissful than negative ones.

To clarify these principles, let's use the analogy of a candle. The closer you are to the flame, the brighter the light will be. Likewise, the closer you are to a permanent state of eternal bliss consciousness, the more you will naturally exhibit positive qualities.

These points aside, pure consciousness remains the ultimate source of all values in life, whether good, neutral, or bad. It is the basis of the universe and all the forms and phenomena contained therein.

Indeed, from a Vedic perspective, there are two aspects of life: (1) pure consciousness in its absolute state, and (2) the manifest world. Pure consciousness is unchanging, whereas the world is ever-changing.

What governs the changes that occur in this world? According to the Vedic tradition, it is the three *gunas*, meaning the forces of creation, maintenance, and destruction. The first *guna*, called *sattva*, is the force of creation; it is associated with purity, harmony, and other positive, life-supporting qualities. Opposite to *sattva* is *tamas*, the force of destruction; it is associated with darkness, ignorance, and stagnancy. Finally, there is *rajas*, the force of maintenance; energetic and active, it supports the other two *gunas*. Sometimes *rajas* upholds *sattva*; at other times, it upholds *tamas*.

These forces can be expressed on a societal level. For example, a peaceful, prosperous society is *sattvic*, whereas a violent, chaotic society is *tamasic*. Whenever *sattva* or *tamas* predominates, then *rajas* must be present, too, maintaining the state of affairs.

We can also speak of these forces on an individual level. For instance, a person may embody *sattvic* traits like positivity and harmony or *tamasic* traits like negativity and destructiveness. Alternatively, they may possess *rajasic*, energetic characteristics like passion and craving.

Naturally, most people have a combination of *sattvic*, *rajasic*, and *tamasic* qualities. So, to assess someone's character, we might ask, "Which *guna* is predominant?" The Bhagavad Gita describes each type of predominance:

> When the light of knowledge shines at every gate in this body, then will one know that sattva is dominant.
>
> Greed, exertion, the undertaking of actions, mental unrest, longing— these arise when rajas dominates, O best of Bharatas.
>
> Absence of illumination, inertness, carelessness and also delusion— these arise when tamas is dominant, O joy of the Kurus.[4]

According to these verses, a person of spiritual knowledge and purity is dominated by *sattva*; a greedy or restless person is dominated by *rajas*; and a careless or deluded person is dominated by *tamas*. (The phrases "O best of Bharatas" and "O joy of the Kurus" refer to Arjuna, the hero of the Bhagavad Gita.)

The quote above parallels the *Star Wars* films. In these films, there is tension between light and darkness, life and death, and peace and violence. Likewise, in Vedic teachings, there is tension between *sattva* and *tamas*. *Sattva* is associated with light, life, and peace, whereas *tamas* is associated with darkness, death, and violence.

But what about *rajas*, the force of maintenance? In some ways, this *guna* is akin to the Force itself. *Rajas* is neutral between *sattva* and *tamas*, just as the Force is neutral between light and darkness. Also, *rajas* is energetic by nature, and the Force is "the energy between all things," to quote Luke.[5]

One may wonder how the Force can be analogous to both *rajas* (the force of maintenance) and *Brahman* (the pure consciousness that underlies and pervades the universe). The answer seems to lie in the following quote, in which George Lucas explains how he came up with the Force: "I began to distill the essence of all religions into what I thought was a basic idea common to all religions and common to primitive thinking."[6] As the filmmaker "distill[ed] the essence of all religions" into a single idea, he probably combined different religious/philosophical principles. In other words, the Force may be an amalgam of diverse concepts; if so, then it is no surprise that it aligns with a variety of teachings.

In fact, comparing the Force to multiple religious/philosophical principles may be helpful; it may reveal nuances of the *Star Wars* philosophy that would otherwise remain hidden. This approach is like examining a foreign object from different angles to better determine its shape.

Let's return to *The Last Jedi*. In this film, Luke admonishes Rey to resist the dark side of the Force. This is a common theme throughout the *Star Wars* movies. But what exactly leads a Jedi into darkness?

THE PATH TO THE DARK SIDE AND ITS VEDIC PARALLELS

When Luke is a young man, the Jedi Master Yoda warns him about the dark side of the Force. Yoda lists three tendencies that can lead a Jedi into darkness: anger, fear, and aggression. Let's consider these qualities from a Vedic perspective.

Like Yoda, Vedic teachers emphasize the harmful effects of anger. For instance, take the following dialogue between Arjuna, the hero of the Bhagavad Gita, and Sri Krishna, his divine mentor:

> Arjuna said: What is it that impels a man to commit sin, even involuntarily, as if driven by force, O Varshneya?

> The Blessed Lord said: It is desire, it is anger, born of rajo-guna, all-consuming and most evil. Know this to be the enemy here on earth.[7]

Clearly, Sri Krishna doesn't mince words; he calls desire and anger "all-consuming and most evil" and "the enemy here on earth."

Now, according to the Vedic teacher Maharishi Mahesh Yogi, desire is not always a bad thing; in fact, it can have a positive, evolutionary effect.[8] This emotion becomes problematic when it keeps us engrossed in the sensory level of life. When this occurs, we fail to experience our true nature, which is eternal bliss consciousness.

As for anger, this emotion has a negative connotation in the Vedic tradition. As Maharishi explains, anger disturbs the natural flow of our desires and impedes our development toward greater happiness.[9] He recommends meditation as a means of cultivating higher states of awareness and thereby reducing irritability, as well as other detrimental tendencies.

Thus, the Vedic tradition and the Jedi have similar perspectives regarding anger.

What about fear, the second trait that Yoda correlates with the dark side of the Force? Vedic teachers also view this emotion in a less-than-positive light. While they don't necessarily consider fear harmful, they do associate it with a lower state of consciousness.

For example, take the following statement from the Brihadaranyaka Upanishad: "Certainly fear is born of duality."[10] According to this quote, fear occurs because one is engrossed in the sensory level of life with its myriad dualities—such as the duality between oneself and a stranger. This perception of two creates a sense of danger since the other person (or animal, or object, etc.) could be a threat.

The Vedic tradition recommends meditation as a means of overcoming fear. Through this practice, we can experience the unity that underlies all duality—namely, eternal bliss consciousness. Over time, this state of awareness can become permanent.

When this happens, the individual no longer has any reason to be afraid. They realize that, deep down, they are immortal. They are one with eternal bliss consciousness, which is—as the name suggests—eternal. To quote the Bhagavad Gita, "These bodies are known to have an end; the dweller in the body is eternal, imperishable, infinite."[11] In other words, although the body dies, the "dweller in the body" (i.e., the inner spirit) lives on. It cannot be damaged or destroyed, so it has nothing to fear. To quote the Bhagavad Gita again, "Weapons cannot cleave him [the inner spirit], nor fire burn him; water cannot wet him, nor wind dry him away."[12] (Here, the use of the gendered term "him" is merely traditional; the inner spirit is beyond gender.)

To recap, meditation can foster awareness of one's immortality, which naturally results in fearlessness. To quote the Bhagavad Gita once more, "Even a little of this dharma [the practice of meditation] delivers from great fear."[13]

As we have seen, both anger and fear have a less-than-positive connotation in the Vedic tradition. So the parallels to Jedi philosophy continue.

What about the third tendency that Yoda warns about—namely, aggression? Vedic teachers also frown on this trait. Indeed, in the great battle that occurs in the Bhagavad Gita, the aggressors are depicted as supporters of evil. The righteous hero, Arjuna, highlights their warlike tendencies in the following verse: "Let me look on those who are assembled here ready to fight, *eager to accomplish in battle* what is dear to the evil-minded son of Dhritarashtra."[14] ("The evil-minded son of Dhritarashtra" refers to Duryodhana, the villainous leader of the enemy army.)

From a Vedic perspective, we can transcend aggressiveness by meditating and experiencing the state of eternal bliss consciousness. The more we are filled with bliss, the more we will naturally act harmoniously.

In summary, both the Jedi and Vedic teachers view anger, fear, and aggression in a less-than-positive light. According to Yoda, these propensities lead "down the dark path."[15] In Vedic terms, these *rajasic* (impassioned) tendencies may have *tamasic* (destructive) effects. For example, anger may cause you to speak harshly to a friend, thereby damaging your relationship.

Now, *rajas* (the force of maintenance) is not always harmful; as discussed earlier, it sometimes upholds *sattva* (the force of creation). For instance, suppose that you work hard to renovate your house. Your action is an expression of *rajas*, but it may give rise to a more *sattvic* (serene) living environment.

What about *tamas* (the force of destruction); does it provide any benefit? How about the dark side of the Force—does it ever serve a greater purpose? Let's consider these topics next.

Chapter 4

BALANCE AND *DHARMA*

In the animated fantasy film *FernGully: The Last Rainforest* (1992), the wise old fairy Magi Lune describes the world in which she lives: "Everything in our world is connected by the delicate strands of the web of life, which is a balance between the forces of destruction and the magical forces of creation."[1] This concept of equilibrium between opposing forces is not new; it is found in ancient Chinese philosophy (in the balance between *yin* and *yang*) and in the Vedic tradition (in the balance between *tamas* and *sattva*—see the previous chapter). This idea is also present in *Star Wars*, in the balance between the dark and light sides of the Force.

BALANCE AND IMBALANCE,
DHARMA AND *ADHARMA*

Let's return to the following statement by Luke Skywalker: "[The Force is] the energy between all things, a tension, a balance, that binds the universe together."[2] Here, the word "balance" suggests that the Force contains opposite values that remain in equilibrium under normal circumstances. As discussed previously, these values include light and darkness, life and death, and peace and violence. Light, life, and peace are creative qualities, while darkness, death, and violence are destructive qualities.

These creative and destructive values play an important role in the functioning of the universe. This is clear from Luke's dialogue with Rey in *The Last Jedi*, in which she refers to "Life. Death and decay, that feeds new life."[3] This quote implies that there is a natural, life-supporting cycle between creation and destruction. This cycle may be seen in a plant that dies and decays, thereby enriching the soil for other plants.

The same basic concepts are found in the Vedic tradition. According to this tradition, the forces of creation (*sattva*) and destruction (*tamas*) are both essential to the evolutionary process.[4] After all, for a new state to be created, the old state must first be destroyed. For example, for lush, new vegetation to grow in a forest, it may be necessary for a fire to destroy the old vegetation.

Under normal circumstances, the creative and destructive forces remain in balance. This is thanks to *dharma*, which the Vedic teacher Maharishi Mahesh Yogi defines as follows:

> Dharma is that invincible power of nature which upholds existence. It maintains evolution and forms the very basis of cosmic life. It supports all that is helpful for evolution and discourages all that is opposed to it.
>
> Dharma is that which promotes worldly prosperity and spiritual freedom.[5]

We see that *dharma* is essential to life; it supports existence and evolution. Here, "evolution" does not refer merely to Darwinian evolution but to progressive development in every sphere of life. The pinnacle of this development is the human attainment of higher states of consciousness, such as yoga and *brahmi chetana*. *Dharma* fosters this spiritual growth, as well as worldly accomplishments.

Dharma furthers these ends by maintaining the balance between the creative and destructive forces. This balance allows for old states to be destroyed and new states to be created in a natural, harmonious way. Under ideal circumstances, each new state will be better than the last, resulting in ever-increasing degrees of "worldly prosperity and spiritual freedom" (to use Maharishi's phrase).[6]

Now, as human beings, we can act either in accordance with *dharma* or against it. In other words, we can behave in a balanced manner that promotes the evolutionary process; alternatively, we can behave in an imbalanced manner that inhibits this process. In either case, we will affect both our personal evolution and the evolution of those around us. For example, if we speak warmly, this will have a positive effect on ourselves and our listeners; if we speak harshly, this will produce the opposite effect.

So what happens when a large portion of society fails to act in a *dharmic* manner? This undermines the power of *dharma*, resulting in an imbalance between the creative and destructive forces. This imbalance hinders the evolutionary process, resulting in widespread suffering.[7] The Vedic term for this situation is *adharma*, meaning "the absence of *dharma*."[8]

The *Star Wars* films also emphasize the dangers of an imbalance between creative and destructive forces (i.e., the light and dark sides of the Force). We see this theme in the prequel trilogy as the Sith begin to gain power and overshadow the light side. The Jedi recognize this threat and cherish the prophecy of an individual who will "bring balance to the Force."[9] They long for a beacon of light to dispel the rising darkness.

The theme of imbalance resurfaces in the original trilogy and the sequel trilogy. In both cases, the Sith have become predominant, and the Jedi are struggling to restore equilibrium. In *The Force Awakens*, the Resistance ally Lor San Tekka describes the bleak situation: "I've traveled too far and seen too much to ignore the despair in the galaxy. Without the Jedi, there can be no balance in the Force."[10] We might put these concepts in Vedic terms: Without the force of creation, there can be no balance in nature. This state of affairs can lead only to suffering and despair.

RESTORING BALANCE: HEROES AND AVATARS

In most of the *Star Wars* films, the dark side of the Force has overpowered the light side. Fortunately, certain individuals—namely, Luke Skywalker, the redeemed Anakin Skywalker, and Rey—counteract this trend and bring balance to the galaxy. In the original trilogy, Luke inspires his father, Anakin, to return to the light side; Anakin, in turn, vanquishes the evil Emperor Palpatine and restores equilibrium to the Force. In the sequel trilogy, the dark side again reigns supreme; however, Rey reestablishes balance by enlivening the spirits of all the Jedi, thus annihilating the emperor once and for all.

These events relate to the Vedic tradition. The Bhagavad Gita also describes times when the force of destruction (*tamas*) overwhelms the force of creation (*sattva*). In these situations, *dharma* has become weak. Again, *dharma* refers to the power of nature that promotes evolution and maintains the balance between the creative and destructive forces (see the previous section). When *dharma* is depleted, *adharma* (the absence of *dharma*) prevails, causing widespread suffering.

In dark times like these, according to Vedic teachings, a special individual called an avatar comes to set things right. Avatars are the direct incarnations of pure consciousness. We encountered one of these figures in the previous chapter: Sri Krishna, who mentors Arjuna in the Bhagavad Gita. Sri Krishna describes his role as follows: "Whenever dharma is in decay and adharma flourishes, O Bharata, then I create Myself. / To protect the righteous and destroy the wicked, to establish dharma firmly, I take birth age after age."[11]

Thus, the function of an avatar is to restore *dharma*, which maintains the balance between the creative and destructive forces. Simplifying this statement a bit, we may say that an avatar's function is to bring balance. This process involves enlivening the force of creation (i.e., protecting the righteous) and mitigating the force of destruction (i.e., destroying the wicked).

In *Star Wars*, Luke, the redeemed Anakin, and Rey fulfill a similar role to the Vedic avatars. First and foremost, these characters bring balance to the Force. They also protect the righteous; Luke and Rey strive to keep their friends safe, and Anakin saves his son's life. Furthermore, these characters destroy the wicked; on separate occasions, both Anakin and Rey vanquish the evil emperor. In summary, the heroes of *Star Wars* essentially do what Vedic avatars do: they restore the proper order of things.

THE FORCE AND *DHARMA*: BINDING
THE UNIVERSE TOGETHER

One last time, let's return to the following quote by Luke: "[The Force is] the energy between all things, a tension, a balance, that binds the universe together."[12] The final phrase—"that binds the universe together"—suggests that the Force is responsible for holding together and maintaining the existence of all things.

From a Vedic standpoint, that's exactly what *dharma* does. The root of this word, *dhr*, means "to hold and bind together."[13] Or, to quote the *Monier-Williams Sanskrit-English Dictionary*, *dhr* means "to hold, bear (also bring forth), carry, maintain, preserve, keep, possess, have, use, employ, practise, undergo."[14] *Dharma* binds together and preserves the universe and everything in it; thus, it plays an identical role to the Force.

One may wonder how the Force can be analogous to both *dharma* and *Brahman*. Before addressing this question, let's consider the relationship between these two Vedic terms. *Brahman* is the source and essence of all things; it encompasses both the unchanging and the ever-changing aspects of life. At the same time, *dharma* maintains the existence of the ever-changing world. You can think of *dharma* as an expression of *Brahman*, just as the waves are the expression of the underlying ocean.

The Force aligns with both *dharma* and *Brahman* because it is essentially a combination of different philosophical concepts.

Let's return to the subject of *dharma*. According to the Vedic tradition, this power of nature doesn't just operate on a cosmic level; it is also relevant on a personal level. Indeed, everyone has their own *dharma*, a path of evolution that is tailored to them. This concept has deep parallels in the *Star Wars* films.

PERSONAL *DHARMA* AND LUKE SKYWALKER'S JOURNEY

From a Vedic perspective, everyone has their own *dharma*, meaning a path of evolution that is ideally suited to them. By following this path, one will ensure the swiftest, smoothest progression toward higher states of consciousness. To attain these states is to reach one's full potential as a human being.

We can think of these evolutionary paths in terms of career; for instance, perhaps it's your *dharma* to be an engineer, whereas it's your partner's *dharma* to be an artist. We can also think of them more broadly in terms of familial roles, hobbies, and/or traditional Vedic practices like yoga and meditation. For example, maybe it's your *dharma* to be a spouse, a parent, a hiker, and a yoga practitioner.

In any case, a person's *dharma* is connected to their innate tendencies. Acting in accordance with these tendencies leads to joy. For instance, if it's your *dharma* to be a banker, then you probably have a strong ability in math and find accounting satisfying. However, if it's your *dharma* to be a teacher, then you are likely a gifted communicator who enjoys sharing knowledge. Of course, you may not recognize your *dharmic* predispositions right away; it can take years to discover the path of evolution that is tailored to you.

Let's delve more deeply into the word *dharma*, which is often translated as "duty." Based on this translation, we may conclude that (1) each of us came into this world with a role to play, and (2) we have an obligation to fulfill that role. As the Vedic teacher Ram Dass (1931–2019) remarks, "You do what you do because that's what the harmony of the universe requires. If I am a potter I make pots."[15] If we fail to follow our *dharma*, it will hamper our spiritual evolution, as well as the evolution of those around us. For instance, if it's our *dharma* to teach, but we refuse to do so, then we probably won't reach our full potential as a human being; furthermore, we will miss the opportunity to foster our students' development.

Although these principles are relevant to modern life, they have been around for thousands of years. Indeed, personal *dharma* is a major theme in the Bhagavad Gita. The hero of this tale, Arjuna, has the *dharma* of a warrior;

it is his natural tendency and responsibility to combat aggressors. He has all
the qualities associated with this evolutionary path, which include "heroism,
vigour, steadiness, resourcefulness . . . generosity and leadership."[16]

Even though Arjuna possesses these traits, he falters when he sees rela-
tives and friends among the ranks of the opposing army. But his mentor,
Sri Krishna, urges him to fulfill his *dharmic* obligation and fight: "Do your
allotted duty."[17] Sri Krishna provides the following nuanced arguments in
favor of this course of action:[18]

1. Everyone on the battlefield is the expression of eternal *Brahman*; as
   such, they are immortal and can never truly perish.
2. This battle is necessary to restore the power of *dharma*, which promotes the evolution of all beings.
3. To quote Sri Krishna, "There is nothing better for a kshatriya [war-
   rior] than a battle in accord with dharma."[19] In other words, there
   is nothing better for a born warrior than having a righteous cause
   to support.
4. Through meditation, one can gain a permanent state of eternal bliss
   consciousness that will remain untouched by any action.

Eventually, Arjuna becomes convinced of Sri Krishna's position, deciding to
fulfill his *dharmic* role in the impending battle.

Let's take a moment to recap a few points about personal *dharma*:

1. *Dharma* is connected to one's innate tendencies.
2. By following one's *dharma*, one may reach their full potential.
3. Everyone has a *dharmic* role to play in this world.

These points have many parallels in *Star Wars*. Let's apply them to
Luke's tale, beginning with the first statement: *Dharma* is connected to one's
innate tendencies.

Luke grows up in a family of farmers, and his uncle, Owen Lars, tries
to keep him involved with this occupation for as long as possible. However,
his aunt Beru points out that he has no affinity for agriculture.

Indeed, Luke is far better suited to becoming a Jedi Knight and Rebel
fighter. First of all, he is strong with the Force, meaning that he has an
intrinsic ability to feel and use this energy field. Second, he is a skilled pilot,
as we see in the battle at the end of *A New Hope*. Third, he is courageous and
loyal, as we observe in many scenes from the original trilogy. All these traits

prove invaluable as Luke rises to confront Darth Vader, hoping to restore balance to the Force.

In short, Luke chooses a path that is tailored to his unique gifts. From a Vedic perspective, he pursues his *dharma*—like the born painter who diligently refines their artistic techniques or the born athlete who strives to excel in sports.

Now let's turn to the second principle listed earlier: By following one's *dharma*, one may reach their full potential.

In the original *Star Wars* trilogy, Luke undergoes significant personal development. For example, let's consider his character arc in *A New Hope*, *The Empire Strikes Back*, and *Return of the Jedi*.

At the beginning of *A New Hope*, Luke is a restless nineteen-year-old who feels trapped by his rural existence. He knows nothing of his extraordinary lineage and has never heard of the Force. Although the boy longs to leave his home planet of Tatooine, he hesitates to join Obi-Wan Kenobi's quest. He agrees to come along only when he discovers that his aunt and uncle have been killed by Imperial stormtroopers.

By the end of *A New Hope*, Luke has evolved a great deal. He has learned to use the Force and helped the Rebels win a major battle against the Empire. He has gained confidence and found a new place in the world.

But Luke has not yet reached his full potential as a Jedi or a human being; he must develop further, as we see in *The Empire Strikes Back*. Although well intentioned, the young man is impatient, with tendencies toward anger and recklessness. For these reasons, Yoda is reluctant to teach him the ways of the Jedi.

Eventually, Yoda gives in. However, Luke's Jedi training is cut short when he has a premonition of his friends in distress. He rushes off to rescue them from the Empire's clutches, confronting Darth Vader in the process. Luke barely survives the encounter; he also receives the shocking news that Vader is his father. He escapes but winds up severely injured and despondent.

Fortunately, Luke soon recovers from his trauma. At the beginning of *Return of the Jedi*, he has come a long way since his clash with Vader. He faces the evil gangster Jabba the Hutt with calmness and confidence. Throughout the confrontation, Luke exhibits impressive Jedi abilities, including mind control, telekinesis, and superhuman agility. When violence becomes unavoidable, he skillfully dispatches his enemies and frees his friends.

Despite these remarkable feats, Luke still has not reached his total potential; he is not even a full-fledged Jedi. To earn this status, he must confront Darth Vader again.

In his final battle with Vader, Luke struggles against the pull of dark emotions like anger, hate, and aggression. At first, he manages to control these feelings; however, he cannot contain himself when the Sith Lord threatens to turn his sister, Princess Leia, to the dark side. At this point, Luke flies into a frenzy; he attacks Vader, forcing him to his knees, cutting off his hand, and holding a lightsaber to his throat. The evil Emperor Palpatine watches with satisfaction, urging the young man to take Vader's place as a Sith Lord.

Then Luke makes his ultimate decision. Rather than giving in to rage, he tosses his lightsaber away and declares that he will never turn to the dark side. At this moment, he truly becomes a Jedi.

Let's consider these events in light of the principles discussed earlier. From a Vedic perspective, it is Luke's *dharma* to become a Jedi. As previously noted, *dharma* promotes spiritual evolution. This point is evident in Luke's journey. By choosing to pursue his natural calling, he makes great progress toward fulfilling his potential as a Jedi and a human being. He transcends the dark side of the Force and establishes himself as an agent of righteousness.

Now let's turn to the third principle listed previously: Everyone has a *dharmic* role to play in this world.

As discussed earlier, in the Bhagavad Gita, it is Arjuna's *dharma* to combat the aggressive Kaurava army. In *Star Wars*, Luke also has an essential role to play: he must save his father's soul.

Why is this so important? Because Luke's father, Anakin, is destined to fulfill an old Jedi prophecy and "bring balance to the Force."[20] Yet he cannot perform this role until he returns to the light side. After all, at the beginning of the original trilogy, Anakin has been Darth Vader for many years; he has embraced the dark side and committed numerous atrocities. Even his old Jedi Master, Obi-Wan, has given up on saving him.

But not Luke. In *Return of the Jedi*, Luke maintains that there is still goodness in Vader, despite all evidence to the contrary. In the end, the young man's courageous actions inspire his father to return to the light side and destroy Emperor Palpatine. Thus, although it is Vader's/Anakin's destiny to restore balance to the Force, Luke is an integral part of this process.

Let's briefly recap the preceding pages. By learning the ways of the Jedi, Luke (1) follows a path that is connected to his innate tendencies, (2) grows toward his full potential as a Jedi and a human being, and (3) performs an essential role in the world—helping restore balance to the Force. In Vedic terms, he follows his *dharma* and reaps the benefits.

Chapter 5

MIND-TO-MIND EFFECTS AND COLLECTIVE CONSCIOUSNESS

"We are all connected." This sentiment appears in a variety of media, from movies to songs to scientific lectures. For instance, in the classic animated film *The Lion King* (1994), King Mufasa tells his son, Simba, that "we are all connected in the great Circle of Life."[1] Similarly, famous astrophysicist Neil deGrasse Tyson (born in 1958) has said, "We're all connected to each other biologically, to the earth chemically, and to the rest of the universe atomically."[2] *Star Wars* and the Vedic tradition also refer to the interconnectedness of all things; however, they address this topic in distinct ways.

MIND-TO-MIND EFFECTS: "THE FORCE IS STRONG WITH THIS ONE!"

In chapter 2, we explored the Vedic principle of *Brahman*, the pure consciousness that theoretically underlies the universe. According to the Upanishads, this cosmic awareness is omnipresent; it is like salt that has dissolved in a bowl of water, permeating every drop.[3] Indeed, *Brahman* pervades and connects all beings and objects.

From a Vedic perspective, because everything is interconnected, every thought, word, and action has an impact on the whole creation. By analogy, if you toss a stone into a pond, the ripples will spread across the entire surface. The Vedic teacher Ram Dass highlights these principles: "Remember, we are all affecting the world every moment, whether we mean to or not. Our actions and states of mind matter, because we are so deeply interconnected with one another."[4]

For the sake of discussion, let's assume these concepts are true. If our thoughts affect the whole universe, then they must affect other living beings, including people. Furthermore, if the people in question are particularly sensitive, then they might sense these mind-to-mind influences.

For example, suppose that you think of an old friend whom you haven't heard from in years; a few minutes later, you receive a call from them. This could be a coincidence; alternatively, it could indicate that your thoughts affected your friend, meaning that the two of you have an unusually deep connection.

To give another example, suppose that a loved one is in peril, and you detect their distress from hundreds of miles away. Although this phenomenon may not have been scientifically verified, there have been many reports of this nature, especially among siblings.

If these examples seem far-fetched, consider this point: Scientific research suggests that it is possible to affect other people directly through meditation. In 1989, scientists Frederick Travis and David Orme-Johnson tested this theory by measuring the brainwave coherence of two subjects.[5] The first subject practiced the Transcendental Meditation technique and an advanced mental technique called the TM-Sidhi program; meanwhile, the second subject did a concept learning task in an adjacent room. Travis and Orme-Johnson found that whenever the brainwave coherence of the meditating individual changed, so did the coherence of the non-meditating individual. The effect was "one way," meaning that the observed changes always occurred first in the meditating subject and then in the non-meditating subject—never the other way around.

Since the two subjects did not interact, Travis and Orme-Johnson concluded that the effect must have occurred via a field of some sort. They proposed the field of pure consciousness described by the Vedic tradition as a possible candidate. According to this line of thinking, the meditating individual "stirred" or enlivened pure consciousness, thereby affecting the other individual at a distance.

A 1997 study revealed similar results. In this experiment, researcher Kurt Warren Kleinschnitz measured the brainwave coherence of a female subject eight times while she practiced the Transcendental Meditation technique.[6] Unbeknownst to the subject, a group of nine graduate students sat in an adjacent room during these meditation sessions. During half of the sessions, they also practiced the Transcendental Meditation technique; during the other half, they studied silently. Kleinschnitz found that the subject exhibited greater brainwave coherence when the students were meditating versus studying. These results suggest that the group meditation created a field effect, which influenced the subject's neurophysiological state. As with the previous study, the researcher proposed that this effect occurred through a field of pure consciousness.

These two studies imply that human consciousness is connected in a way that cannot be explained by Newtonian physics. This connection allows a meditating individual or group to directly affect other people, even when they are in separate spaces.

Let's return to our main point: If everything is connected by pure consciousness, as the Vedic texts claim, then this situation opens the door to mind-to-mind effects, even across distances.

Do these ideas remind you of *Star Wars*? They should! In this fictional universe, everything is connected by the Force. This connection allows the Jedi and the Sith to sense one another's presence, feelings, and intentions, even from far away.

Let's consider an example from *A New Hope*: When Obi-Wan Kenobi secretly enters the Death Star, Darth Vader detects his presence via "a tremor in the Force."[7] Vader even senses Obi-Wan's intentions, realizing that the Jedi is not planning to escape. The Sith Lord shares these observations with Grand Moff Tarkin, the commander of the battle station.

We see another example of a mind-to-mind effect later in the same film when Vader looks toward Luke Skywalker's starship and declares, "The Force is strong with this one!"[8] Although the Sith Lord knows nothing about the young man, he quickly detects Luke's ability to use the Force.

The Jedi also experience mind-to-mind effects through the Force. For instance, in *Return of the Jedi*, Luke feels the conflict between good and evil in Vader's mind, which is why he believes that his father can be redeemed.

For another particularly striking example of a mind-to-mind effect, take Rey and Kylo Ren's long-distance connection in the sequel trilogy. In *The Last Jedi*, the two young adults realize that they can see each other, speak, and touch hands, even though they are located on different planets. In *The Rise of Skywalker*, Kylo takes advantage of this mental link to discover Rey's whereabouts and follow her. He also reveals the source of their unusual bond: He and Rey are a "dyad" in the Force—a mythic concept meaning "two parts of the same whole."[9]

Intriguingly, the mind-to-mind effects in *Star Wars* occur not only across space but also, in some cases, across time. Consider the scene from *The Empire Strikes Back* in which Luke has a vision of his friends Han Solo and Princess Leia in distress. As Yoda explains, the young man is perceiving events that have not yet taken place. This statement implies that the Force transcends time; it is not limited by the past, present, or future.

This concept has profound parallels in the Vedic tradition. According to this tradition, pure consciousness is beyond time. Furthermore, through advanced mental techniques, one may foster "knowledge of the past and future," which is one of the special skills mentioned in the Yoga Sutra.[10] For more on this topic, see the "'Supernatural' Abilities: The Jedi and the Ancient *Siddhas*" section in chapter 2.

To recap, there are many rich examples of mind-to-mind effects in *Star Wars*. According to the philosophy of the Jedi and the Sith, these effects are possible because everything is connected by the Force. By tapping into this universal energy field, Force-sensitive individuals can detect one another's presence, feelings, and intentions, even at a distance.

To further recap, the Vedic tradition also contains the principle that everything is connected. In this case, the source of the connection is *Brahman*, the pure consciousness that underlies and pervades the universe. Moreover, because all things are interrelated, every thought, word, and action affects the whole creation—just as a falling stone creates ripples across the entire pond. This concept provides a theoretical basis for mind-to-mind effects. These effects could range from influencing another person directly through meditation to sensing at a distance that a loved one is in distress.

Let's take the concept that everything is connected a step further by discussing the principle of collective consciousness.

COLLECTIVE CONSCIOUSNESS: "I AM ALL THE JEDI!"

What do you think of when you hear the phrase "collective consciousness"? From a Vedic perspective, this term refers to the combined consciousness of all the individuals in a group. It can apply to any group, small or large; we can speak of the shared awareness of a family, neighborhood, city, state, nation, or even the entire planet. In each case, the group consciousness can be *sattvic*, meaning pure and creative, or *tamasic*, meaning dark and destructive—more on this topic later.[11]

The *Star Wars* films allude to the principle of collective consciousness. For illustration, consider Obi-Wan Kenobi's reaction to the destruction of Alderaan, the planet annihilated by the Empire in *A New Hope*. Although the old Jedi Master is far away from this calamity, he still senses it through the Force. He describes his experience as follows: "I felt a great disturbance in the Force . . . as if millions of voices suddenly cried out in terror and were suddenly silenced. I fear something terrible has happened."[12]

Thus, Obi-Wan feels the collective consciousness of Alderaan's inhabitants; he experiences their fear and deaths as a "great disturbance in the Force." This result suggests that the omnipresent Force connects all people. Sometimes this connection leads to mind-to-mind influences between two individuals, as we saw in the previous section. At other times, it leads to large-scale mind-to-mind effects, allowing individuals like Obi-Wan to sense the consciousness of an entire population.

As previously mentioned, from a Vedic standpoint, collective consciousness can be *sattvic* (meaning pure and creative) or *tamasic* (meaning dark and destructive).

It is easy to apply these concepts to *Star Wars*. For instance, we see both types of collective consciousness in the climax of *The Rise of Skywalker*. First, we observe the *tamasic* type, represented by the spirits of the Sith who surround Rey as she enters Emperor Palpatine's lair. Later, we witness the *sattvic* type, represented by the spirits of the Jedi who uplift Rey in her darkest hour. Let's consider these topics one by one.

When Rey confronts Palpatine, her surroundings are *tamasic*, from the jagged black throne to the ominous chanting of the Sith spirits. The emperor, who embodies all these spirits, is equally *tamasic*. He explains his sinister plan: He wants Rey to become the new embodiment of the Sith's collective consciousness. To quote Palpatine, "Kill me, and my spirit will pass into you, as all the Sith live in me. You will be Empress. We will be one."[13] When Rey refuses to comply, the emperor drains her power, and she collapses; he then attacks the Resistance fleet with streaks of lightning.

Lying on her back, Rey repeatedly murmurs, "Be with me," attempting to connect with the Jedi of the past.[14] She succeeds and hears the voices of Yoda, Qui-Gon Jinn, Obi-Wan Kenobi, Anakin Skywalker, Luke Skywalker, and other deceased Jedi. Together, these spirits typify the *sattvic* type of collective consciousness.

The Jedi say Rey's name and offer words of encouragement: "You're not alone." "Alone, never have you been." "Every Jedi who ever lived, lives in you."[15] These quotes emphasize the theme of collective awareness; they imply that Rey has always been intimately connected to "the Jedi who came before."[16]

Imbued with the spirits' power, Rey rises to challenge the emperor. Palpatine sends a streak of lightning at her, shouting, "You are nothing! A scavenger girl is no match for the power in me! I am all the Sith!"[17] But Rey blocks the attack, countering the Emperor's words: "And I . . . I am all the Jedi!"[18] This dialogue reinforces that Palpatine and Rey embody opposite types of collective consciousness—the negative, *tamasic* type and the positive, *sattvic* type, respectively.

These two types of consciousness may be opposite, but they are not equal; ultimately, the spirits of the Sith are no match for the spirits of the Jedi. This fact becomes clear in the events that follow. Having declared, "I am all the Jedi!" Rey crosses her lightsabers and advances on the emperor. Palpatine's lightning rebounds on her intersected blades, striking his chest and destroying him. Bolts of lightning rain down from above, demolishing the emperor's lair and vanquishing the phantoms of the Sith. In short, light triumphs over darkness.

The Vedic tradition also contains the theme of using light to drive away darkness. Vedic teachers encourage us to enliven *sattva* (which is associated with light and purity) in the collective awareness. But how? First, it is beneficial to meditate and thereby cultivate higher states of consciousness. Second, it is important to choose positive, life-supporting actions. Since everything is interconnected, these approaches will increase *sattva* in our society.

In summary, the principle of collective consciousness is found in both *Star Wars* and the Vedic tradition. These sources discuss positive and negative types of group awareness, promoting the victory of light over darkness.

Chapter 6

DEATH AND IMMORTALITY

What is death? Is it something to be dreaded or accepted? How far should we go to avoid it? Are there worse fates than death? These are relevant questions for any human being to ponder, especially as we grow older.

In modern society, we probably wouldn't answer these questions optimistically since we tend to view death in negative terms. Even if a person has lived a long and fulfilling life, we regard their passing as unfortunate. We constantly seek new ways to extend our time on this earth, from medications to invasive procedures. Some even pursue immortality by having their bodies frozen after death, in the hopes that scientists will eventually discover a way to revive them.[1]

These modern views and approaches conflict with the philosophy of the Jedi, who consider death a natural phenomenon not to be feared. Let's explore this topic and its Vedic parallels.

PERSPECTIVES ON DEATH: "SOON NIGHT MUST FALL"

In *Revenge of the Sith*, Yoda expresses the traditional Jedi view that "death is a natural part of life."[2] He elaborates on this concept in *Return of the Jedi* shortly before his demise: "Twilight is upon me, and soon night must fall. That is the way of things . . . the way of the Force."[3] In other words, death is inevitable, like the coming of night. Yoda betrays no sadness at this thought; instead, he remarks that he has earned his "forever sleep," implying that death is a pleasant reward for the old and weary.[4]

In the Bhagavad Gita, Sri Krishna also emphasizes the inevitability of death. He states, "Certain indeed is death for the born," adding, "Therefore

45

over the inevitable you should not grieve."[5] Simply put, everyone is going to die eventually, so there is no point in lamenting this phenomenon.

Furthermore, according to Sri Krishna, there are worse things than dying. He states, "To a man of honor ill fame is worse than death"[6]; in other words, for a virtuous individual, loss of reputation is more damaging than the loss of life. These principles recall a quote from the 2008 film *The Dark Knight*: "You either die a hero or you live long enough to see yourself become the villain."[7] Better to die as a righteous person than to live a long life tarnished by immoral acts.

In *Star Wars*, Yoda also implies that there are worse things than death, such as turning to the dark side of the Force. This is an important theme in *Revenge of the Sith*. In this film, Anakin Skywalker (later known as Darth Vader) has visions of his secret wife, Padmé Amidala, dying in childbirth. He mentions these premonitions to Yoda, though he leaves out the details. Yoda warns Anakin that "the fear of loss is a path to the dark side," adding that "death is a natural part of life."[8] He instructs the young man not to mourn or miss those who pass away since "attachment leads to jealousy."[9] Clearly, Yoda is more concerned about Anakin's integrity as a Jedi than about any potential death.

Unfortunately, the Sith do not share the Jedi perspective on death; instead, they try to avoid this event at all costs. For instance, take Darth Plagueis "the Wise," who "had such a knowledge of the dark side that he could even keep the ones he cared about from dying."[10] Or take Anakin, who turns to the dark side partially out of his desire to save Padmé's life. Lastly, take Emperor Palpatine, who uses unnatural methods to return to life after he is killed in *Return of the Jedi*.

All three of these characters eventually fail in their efforts to circumvent death. In *Revenge of the Sith*, we learn that Plagueis was murdered in his sleep by his apprentice. In the same film, Padmé dies shortly after Anakin turns to the dark side. And in *The Rise of Skywalker*, Palpatine is vanquished for the second time by Rey.

Anakin's attempt to conquer death comes at a heavy cost: Padmé withdraws from him, devastated by how he has changed. He loses his status among the Jedi and his friendship with his master, Obi-Wan Kenobi. In addition, he winds up severely injured and dependent on his mask and armored suit for survival.

Thus, the *Star Wars* films depict the unfortunate results of trying to cheat death. In this way, they support the Jedi views that (1) "death is a natural part of life"[11] and (2) there are worse things than dying. As previously discussed, these views align with the Bhagavad Gita, which teaches that death is inevitable and preferable to a dishonorable life.

Although the Jedi do not attempt to overcome death, they eventually discover the secret to individual immortality. Let's consider this topic and its Vedic parallels in the next section.

IMMORTALITY AND UNION WITH
THE FORCE/*BRAHMAN*

When we die, do we cease to exist? According to both *Star Wars* and the Vedic tradition, the answer is no. Rather, we carry on in some way—as individual souls and/or through union with the Force/*Brahman*. Let's explore these topics now, beginning with relevant scenes from the *Star Wars* films.

In *Revenge of the Sith*, Yoda discusses the nature of death: "Death is a natural part of life. Rejoice for those around you who transform into the Force."[12] Here, he seems to equate "death" with "transforming into the Force." He appears to be speaking in general terms, which suggests that these statements apply to all people. This would mean that anyone who dies in the *Star Wars* universe becomes one with the Force whether or not they are a Jedi.

The topic of union with the Force crops up again in a deleted scene from the same film.[13] In this scene, Yoda is meditating when he hears the voice of the deceased Jedi Master Qui-Gon Jinn. Qui-Gon reveals that he has discovered the secret to individual immortality. He offers to teach Yoda how to "merge with the Force at will" and retain consciousness after death.[14] Yoda, Obi-Wan Kenobi, and the subsequent Jedi learn this ability.

Of these individuals, Obi-Wan is the first to become immortal; this transition occurs during his clash with Darth Vader in *A New Hope*. At the beginning of the fight, Vader taunts his former master: "Your powers are weak, old man."[15] To which Obi-Wan replies, "You can't win, Darth. If you strike me down, I shall become more powerful than you can possibly imagine."[16] It soon becomes clear what the Jedi Master means. At a critical moment in the skirmish, he calmly allows Vader to slay him. At this moment, Obi-Wan merges with the Force, and his physical form vanishes. Only his cloak remains; it falls to the floor, torn and empty.

Although Obi-Wan's body disappears, his consciousness endures, and he attains remarkable powers. Moments after his passing, he communicates with Luke Skywalker mind to mind, warning the grieving boy to flee from the advancing stormtroopers: "Run, Luke! Run!"[17] Obi-Wan's telepathic abilities continue in subsequent scenes; for instance, in the battle against the Empire, he advises Luke to "use the Force."[18] In *The Empire Strikes Back* and *Return of the Jedi*, Obi-Wan's powers increase; he takes on a visible, shimmering form and holds extended conversations with Yoda and Luke.

Following in the footsteps of Qui-Gon and Obi-Wan, multiple individuals unite with the Force and gain immortality. First, this occurs with Yoda and the redeemed Anakin Skywalker, who both die in *Return of the Jedi* and appear to Luke at the end of this film. Later, it happens to Luke Skywalker and Leia Organa, who pass on in the sequel trilogy and become visible to Rey in *The Rise of Skywalker*.

To recap, in the *Star Wars* universe, all people become one with the Force when they die. The Jedi are also capable of retaining their individual consciousness after death; they use this ability to communicate with the living and influence events in the physical realm.

These concepts have notable parallels in the Vedic tradition. This ancient tradition also refers to individual immortality, as well as the potential for union with an all-pervading field: *Brahman*. Let's consider these principles one by one.

According to the Bhagavad Gita, the spirit of every human being is immortal. To quote Sri Krishna, "These bodies are known to have an end; the dweller in the body is eternal, imperishable, infinite."[19] Simply put, although the body eventually dies, the spirit ("the dweller in the body") lives on.

Elaborating on these concepts, Sri Krishna compares dying to "casting off worn-out garments."[20] The garments symbolize the physiology, which becomes "worn out" through injury or old age; at this point, the spirit casts the body away. This imagery recalls Obi-Wan's cloak, which falls to the ground when he merges with the Force.

Thus, like *Star Wars*, the Vedic tradition contains the principle of individual immortality. Just as death is not an end for Obi-Wan, Yoda, and others, it is also not an end for the warriors in the Bhagavad Gita.

Now, in one respect, *Star Wars* and the Vedic tradition describe individual immortality differently—the Vedic texts include the concept of reincarnation. To quote the Bhagavad Gita, "As the dweller in this body passes into childhood, youth and age, so also does he pass into another body. This does not bewilder the wise."[21] In other words, every spirit will continue taking on new bodies until it becomes established in a higher state of consciousness. There does not seem to be a parallel to this concept in the *Star Wars* films.

Nonetheless, further similarities exist between *Star Wars* and the Vedic texts regarding immortality. For instance, in some ways, becoming one with the Force is analogous to becoming one with *Brahman*.

Becoming one with *Brahman* involves various steps. First, through meditation, one experiences a temporary union with pure consciousness (i.e., the Self). Over time, this unified state of awareness becomes permanent, coexisting with waking, dreaming, and deep sleep. Eventually, one perceives everything that exists as the expression of pure consciousness; this understanding is analogous to realizing that the waves are the expressions of the underlying ocean. In this exalted state of awareness, one recognizes that their essential Self (*Atman*) is the same as the Self of the cosmos (*Brahman*). Thus, they become one with *Brahman* in the fullest sense of the phrase.

Having attained union with *Brahman*, one gains the ultimate immortality. As previously discussed, *Brahman* is everlasting; it is *sat chit ananda*, eternal bliss consciousness. When the individual becomes one with this cosmic awareness, they perceive their immortal nature. They realize that no matter what happens to the body, their consciousness will endure forever. At this point, they do not need to reincarnate; when they die, they simply continue to enjoy the bliss of their own being.

In summary, we might say that there are two types of immortality in the Vedic tradition: (1) the immortality of the individual spirit, which journeys from life to life, and (2) the immortality of union with *Brahman*, which is the goal of life.

The Upanishads frequently mention the second type of immortality. For instance, take the following verse from the Brihadaranyaka Upanishad: "From non-existence lead us to existence, / From darkness lead us to light, / From death lead us to immortality."[22] Here, "nonexistence" refers to the impermanence of material life, whereas "existence" refers to the permanence of union with *Brahman*. Furthermore, "darkness" refers to ignorance, whereas "light" refers to true knowledge (i.e., the knowledge of *Brahman*). Lastly, "death" refers to the demise of the body, whereas "immortality" refers to permanent oneness with *Brahman*. Clearly, in each case, the goal is to go from the lesser value (i.e., nonexistence, darkness, and death) to the greater value (i.e., existence, light, and immortality).

The Isha Upanishad also expresses the desire for eternal existence: "Let this life-breath join with the immortal breath. / Then let this body end in ashes."[23] Like the previous verse, this is a prayer for becoming one with *Brahman* and thereby gaining immortality. Having achieved this goal, the individual does not feel unduly attached to the physical body, which eventually expires; it "end[s] in ashes" through the ritual of cremation. Note that the Jedi also follow this ritual, as we observe in *The Phantom Menace* (when Qui-Gon's body is cremated) and *Return of the Jedi* (when Luke burns his father's armor).

The Vedic principles just discussed have further parallels in the *Star Wars* films. In these films, the characters unite with the all-pervading Force at death. Likewise, in the Vedic tradition, the individual spirit eventually unites with the omnipresent *Brahman*. In both cases, we see a depiction of existence after death and a movement from individuality to universality.

To recap, both *Star Wars* and the Vedic texts express an optimistic view of death; they portray dying as a natural process not to be feared. Both sources also contain the principle of immortality, which takes one of two forms: either (1) the immortality of the individual spirit or (2) the immortality of union with the Force/*Brahman*.

In conclusion, *Star Wars* and the Vedic tradition depict death and immortality similarly, though not identically. Their portrayal of these themes conflicts with the modern perspectives that (1) death is the ultimate end and (2) this outcome should be avoided at all costs.

Note that according to the Advaita Vedanta (nondualistic) school of thought, it is possible to attain union with *Brahman* before death. A person who achieves this goal is known as a *jivanmukta*. The *jivanmukta* continues to live in the world as an individual; however, they never lose awareness of their fundamental Self, eternal bliss consciousness. At death, their body falls away, while their spirit remains one with *Brahman*. There are no clear parallels to the *jivanmukta* in the *Star Wars* films, but similar concepts can be found in the *Star Wars* novels.[24]

Chapter 7

PURPOSE, KARMA, AND RIGHT ACTION

In 2005, Steve Jobs (1955–2011), business magnate and co-founder of Apple Inc., gave the commencement address at Stanford University. In this memorable speech, he discussed "connecting the dots," with each "dot" symbolizing an event in our lives—such as taking a college course or starting our first job. We all want these dots to align and lead in a positive direction, but how can we be sure this will happen? According to Jobs, "You have to trust in something—your gut, destiny, life, karma, whatever." He added, "This approach has never let me down, and it has made all the difference in my life."[1]

Like Jobs, both the Jedi and Vedic teachers trust in something beyond the physical.

PURPOSE AND KARMA: "THERE IS NO SUCH THING AS LUCK"

As noted earlier, when Luke Skywalker first attempts to use a lightsaber to block laser beams, Obi-Wan Kenobi places a helmet over the boy's head that obstructs his vision. The old Jedi Master remarks, "Your eyes can deceive you. Don't trust them. . . . Stretch out with your feelings."[2] Luke follows this advice and succeeds in blocking the beams, even though he can't see anything.

Both Obi-Wan and Han Solo witness this impressive feat; however, they draw different conclusions about it. Obi-Wan attributes Luke's achievement to the Force, whereas Han dismisses it as a matter of luck. The Jedi Master is undaunted by Han's skepticism, commenting, "In my experience, there is no such thing as luck."[3] According to this statement, nothing occurs by chance, which means that everything happens for a reason. In other words, life is inherently purposeful, not random or accidental.

The Jedi are not the only ones to express this view; Vedic teachers agree that our existence is profoundly purposeful. What, then, is its purpose? According to the Upanishads, it is to achieve union with *Brahman*. Ultimately, this means attaining the highest state of human consciousness, in which we spontaneously perceive everything that exists as the expression of our fundamental Self.

Let's suppose that these Vedic teachings are true. It seems clear that some actions will promote our development toward union with *Brahman*, whereas other actions will have the opposite effect. For instance, regular meditation will facilitate our personal growth; by contrast, destructive behavior will stagnate our evolution. In short, if we care about fulfilling the purpose of life, then our actions matter.

Although the Jedi may not discuss the purpose of life in the *Star Wars* films, they agree that our actions matter—hence their determination to embody the light side of the Force and avoid the dark side. So we see a parallel in this regard.

Let's return to the idea that "there is no such thing as luck."[4] From a Vedic perspective, this concept is closely related to karma. Literally, karma means "action"; basically, it refers to the principle that "for every action, there is an equal and opposite reaction" (to quote Sir Isaac Newton's third law of motion).[5] According to this law, every action elicits a corresponding reaction from the universe.

Physicists apply Netwon's third law only to the motion of objects, but Vedic teachers also apply it to matters of right and wrong. From a Vedic standpoint, righteous, evolutionary action ultimately leads to positive results, whereas wrongful, non-evolutionary action leads to negative results.

These principles are analogous to the biblical proverb "As you sow, so shall you reap" (based on Gal. 6:7). This proverb suggests that our actions are like seeds. If we plant vital seeds, we will grow healthy plants; by contrast, if we plant shriveled seeds, we will grow sickly plants. Similarly, honorable actions will produce desirable outcomes, and dishonorable actions will produce undesirable outcomes.

Thus, the Vedic tradition provides a basis for the principle that "there is no such thing as luck"[6]; it asserts that all outcomes are the results of past action. In other words, our previous choices are responsible for our current circumstances. As the Vedic teacher Sadhguru (born in 1957) remarks, "Unless you do the right things, the right things will not happen to you."[7]

We see parallels to these concepts in the *Star Wars* films, which indicate that good will triumph over evil in the end. Consider the climax of the original trilogy: the righteous Luke emerges victorious, while the evil Emperor Palpatine falls to his doom.

For a more complex portrayal of karma, take Anakin Skywalker's storyline. When the young man turns to the dark side, he suffers acutely; his body is largely incinerated, and he is devastated by his wife's passing. However, when Anakin returns to the light side, he is rewarded with immortality; he joins the company of great Jedi like Obi-Wan and Yoda. It seems that Anakin's negative actions lead to negative results, whereas his positive actions lead to positive results.

Now, in *Star Wars*, it often takes a long time for karma to be delivered. For instance, the villainous Emperor Palpatine reigns for decades before his demise. On the other end of the spectrum, the honorable Jedi Master Qui-Gon Jinn is not rewarded for his virtue until the afterlife, when he discovers the secret to individual immortality.

These examples align with the Vedic concept that "karma returns both quickly and slowly."[8] According to this principle, the results of one's actions may come in a day, a month, a year, a decade, or even many lifetimes later (see the discussion of reincarnation in the "Immortality and Union with the Force/*Brahman*" section in chapter 6). Thus, a thief may succeed in stealing a car and yet experience the consequences of this crime in a subsequent life. By contrast, a person who acts generously may earn financial prosperity in a future incarnation.

The *Star Wars* films do not include the concept of reincarnation; however, like the Vedic texts, they do provide a sense of justice after death. After all, it is the righteous Jedi, not the unsavory Sith, who learn how to attain individual immortality.

To recap this section, "there is no such thing as luck"[9] in *Star Wars* or the Vedic tradition. From a Vedic perspective, this concept is based on the principles that (1) life is purposeful, and (2) karma will eventually play out. Although these principles are never stated in *Star Wars*, they seem applicable to the events of the films. So perhaps George Lucas had similar ideas in mind.

If the Vedic teachings are true and karma is real, then choosing right action is of paramount importance. We want to behave in a way that will lead to happiness and not suffering. Yet we may wonder how to discern between right and wrong.

RIGHT ACTION: KNOWING "THE
GOOD SIDE FROM THE BAD"

During *The Empire Strikes Back*, Yoda warns Luke about the dark side of the Force. Luke asks, "But how am I to know the good side from the bad?"[10] The Jedi Master replies, "You will know. When you are calm, at peace. Passive."[11]

Calm, at peace, passive. Does that description sound familiar? It should! After all, the Vedic texts portray pure consciousness as a deeply calm, peaceful, restful state.

That's not to say that Yoda and the Vedic literature are necessarily referring to the same thing. Yoda could be describing a mere mood of calmness. By contrast, the Vedic texts define pure consciousness as a distinct state of awareness beyond the ordinary states of waking, dreaming, and deep sleep.

Still, there is a parallel here: both Yoda and Vedic teachers consider inner peace the proper basis for right action. Let's explore this principle from a Vedic perspective.

Naturally, the more serene we are, the less our perception is tainted by negative emotions. It is easier to keep things in perspective when we start from a baseline of peacefulness versus agitation. A relaxed state of mind can give us greater clarity in assessing complex situations, especially matters of right and wrong.

Suppose that our calmness comes from accessing the state of pure consciousness. If so, then this transcendental experience will directly cause us to act in a more evolutionary manner. As discussed in chapter 2, pure consciousness (i.e., *Brahman*) is the source of the universe. It contains infinite intelligence, through which it governs the world in a positive, life-supporting direction. When we unite with this universal awareness through meditation, we awaken its intelligence within ourselves. Therefore, we spontaneously begin to think and act in a more orderly, creative, and progressive way. We start to behave in a manner that promotes happiness and reduces suffering. For instance, we might find a peaceful resolution to a contentious work situation.

Thus, the state of pure consciousness naturally gives rise to right action. Here, "right action" means "evolutionary action"—behavior that promotes growth toward higher states of consciousness for both oneself and others.

In summary, Yoda and Vedic teachers believe a calm, peaceful state of awareness is the ideal basis for right action. This concept recalls the conventional wisdom of taking a deep breath and counting to ten before dealing with a frustrating situation. Although this approach probably won't bring you to pure consciousness, it may improve your state of mind and keep you from overreacting.

Chapter 8

INTUITION AND NON-ATTACHMENT

In his 2005 commencement address at Stanford University, business magnate Steve Jobs gave the graduating students the following advice: "Don't let the noise of others' opinions drown out your own inner voice. And most important, have the courage to follow your heart and intuition."[1]

These ideas are not new; they can be found in a variety of sources, from ancient texts to modern films. Both the Vedic literature and the *Star Wars* movies depict the value of listening to your intuition.

INTUITION: "SEARCH YOUR FEELINGS"

The theme of intuition comes up often in *Star Wars*. For example, consider Luke Skywalker's remark when he sees the Death Star in *A New Hope*: "I have a very bad feeling about this."[2] Although the boy has never heard of the Imperial battle station, he just knows that the moonlike structure in front of him means trouble. Other characters repeat Luke's line with minor variations throughout the Skywalker saga. In each case, the speaker correctly senses that danger is approaching. Their insights are not based on intellectual analysis, but rather on instinct or a gut feeling.

Another well-known *Star Wars* quote—"Search your feelings"—is basically a prompt to listen to one's intuition. This expression also appears in multiple films. In *The Empire Strikes Back*, Emperor Palpatine uses these words to convince Darth Vader that he (Vader) is Luke's father: "Search your feelings, Lord Vader. You will know it to be true."[3] Later in the same film, Vader uses the same phrase to break the news to Luke: "I am your father. . . . Search your feelings. You know it to be true."[4] Lastly, in *Return of the Jedi*,

Luke borrows this expression to remind Vader of his true nature: "Search your feelings, Father. . . . I feel the conflict within you. Let go of your hate."[5] In each instance, this phrase is used to appeal to the listener's intuition as opposed to their intellect.

Just as intuition helps convince Luke that Vader is his father, it also reveals to him that Princess Leia is his sister. This topic comes up during a conversation between Luke and the spirit of Obi-Wan Kenobi in *Return of the Jedi*. Obi-Wan informs the young man that he has a twin sister. Luke briefly protests and then correctly guesses his sibling's identity. He does not go through a lengthy reasoning process to arrive at this conclusion; rather, he instinctively senses the truth.

Leia is equally intuitive. When Luke informs her that they are siblings, she replies, "I know. Somehow . . . I've always known."[6] This is an impressive level of insight, given that the twins grew up on different planets without ever hearing about each other.

In summary, intuition is an important theme in *Star Wars*. This faculty of perception seems related to the Force; it is generally the Force-sensitive characters, like the Jedi and the Sith, who demonstrate intuitive tendencies. These characters use the all-pervading energy field to discover hidden knowledge about themselves and others.

These concepts have strong parallels in the Vedic tradition. According to this tradition, through meditation, one may transcend the surface of the mind and enjoy deeper, more refined levels of awareness. The most profound level is pure consciousness, which the Yoga Sutra describes as follows: "There resides the intellect that knows only the truth."[7] In other words, by experiencing this unified state of awareness, one gains access to the truth. After all, in the Advaita Vedanta (nondualistic) school of thought, pure consciousness/*Brahman* is the source of the entire universe; as such, it contains all knowledge. This discussion brings to mind the following quote from the Vedic teacher Sadhguru: "The most incredible thing is that you can know everything you wish to know with your eyes closed."[8]

At first, the state of pure awareness is fleeting, but, through regular meditation, it can become permanent. When this occurs, the individual has lasting access to the truth; they can find the answer to any question by looking within. To quote the Yoga Sutra again, "Through intuition everything can be known."[9]

Now, according to Vedic teachings, intuition is not to be confused with everyday emotions. For example, intuition may guide you toward a particular career path, but it is probably not responsible for your desire to gorge on chocolate cake! In all likelihood, a more superficial level of the mind gave rise to that craving. Ultimately, intuition promotes development toward higher states of consciousness, whereas ordinary emotions can hinder this evolutionary process.

The *Star Wars* films also seem to distinguish between intuition and everyday emotions. In these movies, emotions like fear and anger often lead to misfortune, whereas intuition provides a solid basis for action. We see an example of the former scenario in *The Empire Strikes Back* and an example of the latter scenario in *Return of the Jedi*. Let's consider these films now.

The Empire Strikes Back demonstrates the pitfalls of acting from a state of emotional turmoil. In this film, Luke makes an impassioned decision to rescue his friends from Darth Vader, even though Yoda and Obi-Wan Kenobi warn that he is not ready for the conflict. Sure enough, the young man's reckless actions almost lead to his ruin.

By contrast, *Return of the Jedi* illustrates the value of following one's intuition. In this film, Luke correctly senses that there is still good in his father, despite all evidence to the contrary; therefore, he aims to bring Vader back to the light side of the Force. The young man succeeds in his undertaking, which validates his insight into his father's true nature.

To recap, both *Star Wars* and the Vedic tradition depict the power of intuition. Furthermore, both sources seem to distinguish between intuition and superficial emotions (at least implicitly in the case of *Star Wars*). Lastly, both sources refer to an all-pervading reality that underlies intuition: the Force/*Brahman*.

NON-ATTACHMENT: "ATTACHMENT LEADS TO JEALOUSY"

Why does Anakin Skywalker turn to the dark side of the Force? As discussed in the "Perspectives on Death: 'Soon Night Must Fall'" section in chapter 6, he does so partially out of attachment to his secret wife, Padmé Amidala. Early in *Revenge of the Sith*, Anakin has premonitions of Padmé's demise; therefore, he seeks Sith knowledge of how to prevent death. His quest drives him to become the apprentice of the evil Chancellor Palpatine.

Although Anakin's desire to save Padmé's life is understandable, his degree of attachment to her seems unhealthy. Certainly, Yoda would agree. In *Revenge of the Sith*, the old Jedi Master warns Anakin about the harmful effects of attachment, stating, "The fear of loss is a path to the dark side," "Attachment leads to jealousy," and, referring to jealousy, "The shadow of greed that is."[10] Let's consider these statements one by one.

"The fear of loss is a path to the dark side": Vedic teachers would concur that clinging to anything impermanent, such as a loved one on the brink of death, can lead only to suffering and spiritual darkness.[11]

"Attachment leads to jealousy": Here, "jealousy" does not appear to mean "envy"; instead, it seems to refer to being "fiercely protective or vigilant of one's rights or possessions."[12] In fact, Anakin treats Padmé like a cherished possession, determined to protect her no matter the cost. Yet Padmé is not a possession. From a Vedic standpoint, she is a distinct *jiva* or spirit; she has her own karma and *dharma* (evolutionary path), which Anakin should not try to control.

"[Jealousy is the] shadow of greed": "Greed" means the "intense and selfish desire for something."[13] Again, this discussion recalls Anakin's habit of treating Padmé like a prized possession.

To help Anakin escape from fear, attachment, and jealousy, Yoda offers the following advice: "Train yourself to let go of everything you fear to lose."[14] The theme of letting go appears in other *Star Wars* films as well.

In *A New Hope*, when Luke is trying to block laser beams with a lightsaber, Obi-Wan says, "This time, *let go* your conscious self and act on instinct."[15] In other words, Luke should temporarily abandon his sense of individuality and act spontaneously. Doing so will help him use the all-pervading Force to his advantage.

In the climax of the same film, the theme of letting go comes up again. Obi-Wan's disembodied voice instructs Luke to "use the Force" to destroy the Death Star.[16] Luke hesitates, tempted by the computerized targeting device. But Obi-Wan persists: "Let go, Luke. . . . Luke, trust me."[17] So the boy lets go of his reliance on his senses, turning off the targeting device. More profound, he lets go of trying to control the situation, trusting that, through the Force, he will make the right move. As a result, he is able to release the "one in a million" shot that annihilates the Death Star.[18]

The concept of letting go also comes up in *Return of the Jedi* when Luke confronts Vader. Convinced there is still goodness in Vader, Luke tries to reach him with the following words: "Search your feelings, Father. . . . I feel the conflict within you. *Let go* of your hate."[19] In other words, Vader should let go of his raw emotions and remember his true self. He should let go of the limitations of being Darth Vader and instead embrace the possibilities of being Anakin Skywalker, the Jedi destined to bring balance to the Force.

In summary, attachment and letting go are important themes in the *Star Wars* films. Attachment is partially responsible for luring Anakin to the dark side. By contrast, through letting go, Luke learns to use the Force, and his father returns to the light side.

The Vedic tradition also emphasizes the harmful effects of attachment. According to the Yoga Sutra, this psychological tendency is one of the main causes of suffering.[20] In addition, it is an obstacle to spiritual growth. "Those obstacles that distract the mind are disease, fatigue, doubt, careless-ness, laziness, *attachment*, confused understanding, failure to achieve *samādhi* and failure to maintain *samādhi*."[21] (*Samādhi* means "transcendence," or the state of yoga.)

How can attachment be avoided? According to the Vedic teacher Maharishi Mahesh Yogi, the key is to meditate and experience the state of eternal bliss consciousness (*sat chit ananda*). Through regular practice, this state can become permanent. At this point, the individual is so filled with bliss that they are not attached to anything. After all, why cling to the happiness that external objects bring when you have an unbounded reser-voir of joy within? Or, to borrow one of Maharishi's analogies, why crave sweet foods when you already have the intense sweetness of saccharine on your tongue?

That's not to say that an individual in a permanent state of eternal bliss consciousness will be indifferent toward people, objects, or situations. On the contrary, they will naturally desire "the welfare of the world."[22] Their altruistic perspective will be reflected in their actions, which will be friendly, loving, and generous.

Still, no matter what happens, it will be insufficient to disturb the individual's inner state of bliss. In the words of the Bhagavad Gita, this for-tunate person has "gained equanimity in pleasure and pain, in gain and loss, in victory and defeat."[23] Their peaceful, balanced state of consciousness will persist regardless of external circumstances.

The Yoga Sutra describes this state as follows: "In the state of non-attachment one is freed from desire for objects, whether seen or heard of. This is the indication of the triumph of the Self."[24] In other words, when one gains union with the Self (i.e., eternal bliss consciousness), one is freed from all cravings. According to Maharishi, although one still experi-ences desires, they are no longer strong enough to overshadow one's bliss. Moreover, these impulses are evolutionary, having a positive impact on the surrounding environment. For example, one might have the desire to cook a meal to share with friends.

The Yoga Sutra elaborates on non-attachment: "The highest state of non-attachment is freedom from all change, which comes through knowledge of the Self."[25] In other words, through union with the Self, one realizes one's eternal, unchanging nature. In this way, one gains "freedom from all change." Obviously, on the surface, they will continue to develop and have new experiences. Nonetheless, deep down, they will remain the same blissful Self.

It's important to note that, according to Maharishi, non-attachment is not a matter of *trying* to be detached. He considers this an unnatural and harmful impulse. After all, from a Vedic standpoint, life is meant to be enjoyed, not rejected. So, the basis of non-attachment should be an inner state of bliss, not a contrived mood of indifference.

This state of bliss is also the basis for "letting go"—a theme that appears in multiple *Star Wars* films (see the discussion earlier in this section). From a Vedic perspective, we need to let go of attachment, individual limitations, and the ignorance of our true nature. We can achieve these goals by enlivening the state of eternal bliss consciousness through meditation. Fulfilled by this experience, we will naturally stop clinging to temporary objects and situations.

In summary, both *Star Wars* and the Vedic tradition place great value on non-attachment, encouraging us to let go of our individual limitations. One might wish that Anakin had learned a traditional Vedic style of meditation. If he had, perhaps he could have transcended his unhealthy attachment to his wife, as Yoda would have wanted. Fortunately, in the end, Anakin lets go of his destructive tendencies and returns to the light side of the Force.

Chapter 9

KNOWLEDGE AND STRENGTH OF MIND

Gary Player (born in 1935), widely considered one of the greatest golfers of all time, has stated, "A strong mind is one of the key components that separates the great from the good."[1] Chrissie Wellington (born in 1977), a four-time Ironman Triathlon World Champion, expressed a similar idea: "It's when the discomfort strikes that they realize a strong mind is the most powerful weapon of all."[2]

Do these statements remind you of Jedi teachings? They should! Both *Star Wars* and the Vedic tradition depict the power of a strong mind.

STRONG-MINDEDNESS AND WEAK-MINDEDNESS

In a famous scene from *A New Hope*, an Imperial stormtrooper questions Luke Skywalker about the droids in his possession (namely, C-3PO and R2-D2). Obi-Wan Kenobi gestures with his hand and tells the trooper, "These aren't the droids you're looking for."[3] Surprisingly, the trooper is immediately convinced by Obi-Wan's statement, echoing his words and allowing Luke to pass by without further inspection. Shortly thereafter, the boy expresses confusion about the incident. Obi-Wan replies, "The Force can have a strong influence on the weak-minded."[4] Thus, he reveals that he used a Jedi mind trick on the trooper.

Other *Star Wars* scenes explore the theme of weak-mindedness and its opposite, which we might call strong-mindedness. Take the scene in *The Force Awakens* in which Kylo Ren tries to read Rey's mind. Initially, he succeeds, but then Rey realizes she can resist his attempts. She even turns the tables on Kylo, momentarily reading his mind instead. Later, she uses the

Force to convince a guard to release her from imprisonment. Both incidents demonstrate Rey's remarkable strength of mind.

These subjects relate to the Vedic tradition, which teaches that enlightened individuals are strong-minded (i.e., they remain steady and resolute regardless of external circumstances). These individuals have "equanimity in pleasure and pain, in gain and loss, in victory and defeat."[5] Due to their balanced state of mind, they are unlikely to be manipulated by others.

If the enlightened are strong-minded, then, by comparison, the unenlightened are weak-minded. The Bhagavad Gita elaborates: "He who is not established [in the state of pure consciousness] has no intellect, nor has he any steady thought. The man without steady thought has no peace; for one without peace how can there be happiness?"[6] According to this verse, unenlightened individuals lack discernment and steadiness of thought; as a result, they are not fully peaceful or joyful. The statement "He . . . has no intellect, nor has he any steady thought" recalls the stormtrooper discussed earlier in this section, who is susceptible to Obi-Wan's mind trick.

The Vedic tradition also refers to the possibility of gaining "knowledge of another's mind,"[7] which is analogous to Rey reading Kylo Ren's thoughts. From a Vedic standpoint, this ability would stem from experiencing union with pure consciousness, the most fundamental level of life, and then acting from that level.

In summary, the *Star Wars* concepts of strong-mindedness and weak-mindedness have notable parallels in the Vedic tradition.

Now, the Jedi sometimes use their mental strength to attain knowledge, such as when Rey reads Kylo Ren's thoughts. Vedic teachers also place importance on knowledge.

KNOWLEDGE AND IGNORANCE: "YOU MUST UNLEARN WHAT YOU HAVE LEARNED"

Both the Jedi and Vedic teachers cherish knowledge, passing along key principles from generation to generation. Some of these principles are practical, dealing with topics like lifting objects (in *Star Wars*) or preventing disease (in the Vedic tradition). Others are more profound, relating to the nature of life or immortality (subjects found in both *Star Wars* and the Vedic texts).

Referring to these deeper principles, the Bhagavad Gita states, "Truly there is in this world nothing so purifying as knowledge."[8] From a Vedic perspective, knowledge allows the individual to discern between the world, which is transient, and the Self (i.e., pure consciousness), which is eternal. This viewpoint "purifies" the Self by revealing its true, unbounded nature.

Of course, gaining knowledge involves overcoming ignorance, which is a central theme in both *Star Wars* and the Vedic tradition.

For instance, take *The Empire Strikes Back*, in which Yoda trains Luke to become a Jedi. In this film, the young man succeeds in using the Force to lift rocks, and yet he doubts that it is possible to lift his starship out of the swamp in the same way. He asserts that these two tasks are "totally different." Yoda replies, "No! No different! Only different in your mind. You must unlearn what you have learned." Luke then tries to think the ship out of the swamp, but he fails. Panting, he states, "I can't. It's too big." Once again, Yoda corrects his words: "Size matters not." The Jedi Master explains that Luke needs to "feel the Force" between all things, including the land and the ship.[9] But the young man gives up, so Yoda lifts the ship out instead.

This scene depicts the limitations created by ignorance. Luke is trapped in a physical mindset, thinking that large objects are harder to lift than small objects. But the Force permeates all things, so as long as a Jedi uses this energy field, they can move anything. Until Luke internalizes this idea, he will continue to struggle.

For another example of the importance of overcoming ignorance, take the scene from *A New Hope* in which Luke learns to wield a lightsaber. As discussed earlier, he struggles to use this weapon to block laser beams emitted by a hovering robot. Obi-Wan places a helmet over the boy's head that obstructs his vision. The Jedi Master cautions Luke not to trust his eyes, as they may deceive him. In other words, the boy should stop relying on his physical senses; instead, he should use the Force. Luke follows this advice and succeeds in blocking the laser beams.

Based on this scene, we can say that it is a form of ignorance to depend solely on eyesight or other physical senses. Instead, a knowledgeable Jedi will rely primarily on the Force.

Vedic teachers agree that the physical senses can be deceptive. When a person is engrossed in the sensory level of life, they perceive the diversity of the world and yet miss the underlying unity of pure consciousness. This situation is like seeing waves but failing to notice the ocean beneath. It is the most basic form of ignorance.

The Yoga Sutra elaborates: "Ignorance is perceiving the non-eternal as eternal, the impure as pure, suffering as happiness, and the non-Self as Self."[10] Perceiving "the non-eternal as eternal" and "the impure as pure" means viewing the world as permanent and absolute; in reality, these descriptors apply only to pure consciousness. Perceiving "suffering as happiness" means mistaking earthly pleasures for the unbounded bliss of higher states of awareness. Lastly, perceiving "the non-Self as Self" means identifying with the physical rather than realizing one's true nature as pure consciousness.

The Bhagavad Gita also comments on the nature of ignorance:"Wisdom is veiled by ignorance.Thereby creatures are deluded."[11] This verse describes the confused and unfulfilling existence of most human beings. Fortunately, there is still hope for us, as indicated by the next verse: "But in those in whom that ignorance is destroyed by wisdom, wisdom, like the sun, illumines That which is transcendent."[12] In other words, to remove ignorance, all we need to do is enliven knowledge, especially the knowledge of the transcendent (pure consciousness).This is like eliminating darkness by introducing light.

The Upanishads comment on the topic of ignorance as well. Consider the following statement from the Shvetashvatara Upanishad: "Ignorance is perishable, knowledge is immortal."[13] In other words, false perceptions do not last; only the truth endures forever. The Mundaka Upanishad expresses a similar theme: "Truth alone triumphs."[14] In 1950, this statement became the national motto of India.

For an illustration of the principle that "truth alone triumphs," think of paradigm shifts in science. For example, scientists eventually realized that the sun, not the earth, is the center of our solar system. They also became aware of the limitations of classical mechanics and adopted more advanced theories, such as the theory of relativity and quantum mechanics. In each of these cases, the old theory lingered for hundreds of years; nonetheless, in the end, a more accurate understanding came to light. These examples support the Vedic teaching that, sooner or later, the truth will prevail.

To recap, both *Star Wars* and the Vedic tradition highlight the importance of overcoming ignorance. In *Star Wars*, Luke must unlearn what he has learned; he must stop thinking of the world in solely physical terms and recognize that the Force permeates all things. Likewise, in the Vedic tradition, one must transcend the limitations of the senses; one must realize that pure consciousness underlies all diversity, just as the ocean underlies the crashing waves.

Now, from a Vedic perspective, it is not enough to grasp this truth intellectually; you also need to experience it firsthand through meditation. By analogy, to fully understand what an apple is like, it is not sufficient to read about this type of fruit; you also need to eat one.

Indeed, the Vedic texts value both knowledge and experience. The Shvetashvatara Upanishad urges the reader to "fathom / that source [pure consciousness] through knowledge (*samkhya*) and experience (*yoga*)."[15] Similarly, in the Bhagavad Gita, Sri Krishna states, "That Yogi is said to be united who is contented in knowledge and experience."[16] In other words, through the knowledge and experience of pure consciousness, one gains permanent union with the Self. Sri Krishna elaborates: "I shall declare to you without reserve this knowledge combined with experience. Once this is known nothing else remains worth knowing in this world."[17] That is to say, all worldly knowledge pales in comparison to the knowledge and experience of pure consciousness.

Like Sri Krishna, the Jedi value experience as well as knowledge. Take the *Star Wars* scenes discussed earlier in this section. In *The Empire Strikes Back*, Yoda informs Luke that he must "feel the Force" between all things, including the land and the starship.[18] Likewise, in *A New Hope*, Obi-Wan tells the boy to stretch out with his feelings. Clearly, it is not sufficient for Luke to believe in the Force; he must also feel, or experience, this energy field firsthand.

Let's return to the topic of knowledge. Although knowledge can be acquired from external sources, it can also be attained from within. The *Star Wars* quote "Search your feelings" illustrates this point; it implies that a Force-sensitive individual can obtain information simply by listening to their intuition.

The theme of gaining knowledge from within brings to mind a scene from *The Last Jedi*. In this scene, the spirit of Yoda burns down the tree that supposedly contains the sacred Jedi texts. When the aged Luke protests, Yoda acknowledges that these texts held wisdom; however, he states, "That library contained nothing that the girl Rey does not already possess."[19] Here, Yoda seems to be speaking literally, knowing that Rey took the books before he destroyed the tree (as the audience later discovers). However, he could also be speaking figuratively, implying that the young woman has all the wisdom she needs within herself.

We find a similar concept in the following verse from the Bhagavad Gita: "To the enlightened brahmin [scholar] all the Vedas are of no more use than is a small well in a place flooded with water on every side."[20] According to this verse, an enlightened individual does not need the Vedic texts because they already have all the wisdom they require within themselves. Further study is unnecessary, just as a well is unnecessary in a place that is inundated with water.

In summary, the Jedi and Vedic teachers share the following views regarding knowledge: (1) it is immensely valuable; (2) it can be gained from within; (3) it should be supplemented by experience; and (4) the opposite of knowledge—namely, ignorance—must be overcome.

Chapter 10

OUR TRUE NATURE

What are we fundamentally? Are we our bodies? Our mental processes? Our social identities? According to *Star Wars* and the Vedic tradition, we are more than any of these things. Both of these sources provide a deep and rich description of our true nature.

BEYOND MATTER: "LUMINOUS BEINGS ARE WE"

In *The Empire Strikes Back*, Yoda describes our essential nature: "Luminous beings are we . . . not this crude matter."[1] Clearly, from a Jedi perspective, we are more than our bodies. This idea recalls the following statement (which is of uncertain origin): "You are not a human being having a spiritual experience. You are a spiritual being having a human experience."[2]

Vedic teachers agree that we are nonphysical beings who have temporarily taken physical form. Our bodies are like clothes; we use them for a while and then discard them when they become ragged. Indeed, in the Bhagavad Gita, Sri Krishna compares dying to "casting off worn-out garments."[3] As this analogy suggests, our inner spirit survives death. To quote Sri Krishna again, "These bodies are known to have an end; the dweller in the body is eternal, imperishable, infinite."[4]

Ultimately, from a Vedic perspective, our inner spirit is identical to pure consciousness. We can experience the union of our individual self with the universal Self through traditional Vedic styles of meditation. This union occurs when we transcend all thoughts, emotions, and perceptions. To quote the Yoga Sutra, "Yoga is the complete settling of the activity of the mind. Then the observer is established in the Self."[5] In other words, when all mental activity has faded away, the meditator becomes one with the Self.

As previously discussed, the Self is eternal bliss consciousness (*sat chit ananda*). To quote the Katha Upanishad, it is "unchanging, eternal . . . without beginning or end."[6] To quote the Mundaka Upanishad, it is "shining, full of bliss."[7] Lastly, to quote the Katha Upanishad again, it is "the consciousness in conscious beings."[8]

In summary, according to both the Vedic tradition and *Star Wars*, our true nature is nonphysical. Therefore, if we think of ourselves only in terms of our bodies, we are severely limiting ourselves.

As nonphysical beings, how should we engage with the world? From a Vedic standpoint, we want to be positive and selfless in our thoughts, words, and actions. The Jedi hold similar views.

POSITIVITY AND SELFLESSNESS

In *The Empire Strikes Back*, when Luke Skywalker's starship sinks into the swamp, he and Yoda have different perspectives on the situation. Luke's view is negative, as illustrated by his declaration that "we'll never get [it] out now" and other similar comments.[9] By contrast, Yoda's view is positive since he knows all things are possible through the Force.

These different perspectives lead to different outcomes. Luke fails to Force-lift the ship from the swamp, whereas Yoda completes this task with ease. The young man witnesses this impressive feat and states, "I don't . . . I don't believe it." The Jedi Master replies, "That is why you fail."[10]

These events depict the power of positivity: Yoda's optimism brings success, while Luke's pessimism results in failure. Clearly, the young man needs to learn to view the world in a more hopeful light.

The Vedic tradition contains similar themes. It encourages us to focus on the positive, as illustrated by this verse from the Rig-Veda: "All good I should hear from the ears. All good I should see through the eyes."[11] This tradition also urges us to avoid negativity, as evidenced by the following excerpt from the Upanishads of Krishna Yajur-Veda: "Let us be together, / Let us eat together, / Let us be vital together, / Let us be radiating truth, / radiating the light of life, / Never shall we denounce anyone, / never entertain negativity."[12]

The Vedic teacher Paramahansa Yogananda (1893–1952) echoes these themes in the following statement: "If you permit your thoughts to dwell on evil, you yourself will become ugly. Look only for the good in everything, that you absorb the quality of beauty."[13]

From a Vedic standpoint, in any state of consciousness, it is possible to choose to focus on the positive. However, if we cultivate higher states of awareness through meditation, then our attention will *naturally* flow in a positive direction. After all, these states are characterized by inner bliss, which makes it easier to appreciate the world around us.

In summary, both *Star Wars* and the Vedic tradition encourage positivity.

Let's turn to the second topic mentioned above: selflessness. The Jedi encourage us to be selfless in our actions. To quote Anakin Skywalker's words to Chancellor Palpatine in *Revenge of the Sith*, "The Jedi are selfless. . . . They only care about others."[14] We see many examples of Jedi who risk their lives to serve a greater cause, including Yoda, Qui-Gon Jinn, Obi-Wan Kenobi, Luke Skywalker, the redeemed Anakin Skywalker, and Rey. Four of these individuals die as a result of their heroic acts: Qui-Gon, Obi-Wan, Anakin, and, eventually, Luke.

Vedic teachers value selflessness as well.[15] They promote meditation, which can help us become less attached to the individual self and more grounded in the universal Self. Through this evolutionary process, we naturally develop a cosmic perspective and begin to desire "the welfare of the world."[16] This perspective is reflected in our actions, which become friendly, loving, and generous.

When we attain the pinnacle of Self-realization (i.e., *brahmi chetana*, or Unity Consciousness[17]), we spontaneously perceive all beings as the expressions of our own pure consciousness. To quote the Bhagavad Gita, "[The fully enlightened individual] sees the Self in all beings, and all beings in the Self."[18] This perspective creates a profound sense of familiarity with all people and creatures. The following verse from the Maha Upanishad captures this feeling: "The world is my family."[19]

One can easily imagine the Jedi voicing a similar sentiment—for example, "The galaxy is my family." After all, they care deeply about the welfare of the galactic citizens; that is why they strive to maintain "peace and justice" throughout their world.[20]

Thus, both the Jedi and Vedic teachers place importance on selflessness.

Now, what happens when an individual acts selfishly for an extended period of time? Is there hope for such a person?

REDEMPTION AND HIGHER STATES
OF CONSCIOUSNESS

In *Star Wars*, the Sith act selfishly and immorally, pursuing their desires and harming anyone who stands in their way. As a result, they eventually receive negative karma.

However, there is the possibility of redemption if one turns away from the dark side of the Force. Indeed, after years of evildoing, both Anakin Skywalker (aka Darth Vader) and Ben Solo (aka Kylo Ren) return to the light side and achieve salvation.

Anakin's and Ben's true, virtuous selves were there all along, hidden under the surface. Luke makes this point to Anakin in *Return of the Jedi*: "It [Anakin Skywalker] is the name of your true self. You've only forgotten. I know there is good in you. The Emperor hasn't driven it from you fully."[21] Rey makes the same point to Ben in *The Rise of Skywalker* by using his given name, not his dark alias.

We find similar themes in the Vedic tradition. The Vedic version of redemption is the attainment of higher states of consciousness, especially *brahmi chetana* (Unity Consciousness[22]). In this state, one has transcended all immoral tendencies. Anyone can achieve this goal, as indicated by the following verse from the Bhagavad Gita: "Even if you were the most sinful of all sinners, you would cross over all evil by the raft of knowledge alone."[23] In other words, even the worst person imaginable could find redemption through the knowledge and experience of *brahmi chetana* (which is gained through meditation).

From a Vedic perspective, our true Self is always within us, whether or not we are aware of it. It is like the sun, which is always present, even when hidden behind clouds. Furthermore, the Self is beyond all evil. Thus, redemption is simply a matter of enlivening our essential nature; it is like blowing away the clouds to allow the sun to shine.

In summary, both *Star Wars* and the Vedic tradition contain the principle of redemption. In *Star Wars*, Anakin Skywalker and Ben Solo are redeemed by returning to their true, virtuous nature. Likewise, in the Vedic tradition, we are redeemed by reconnecting with our essential Self, which is beyond immorality.

Thus far, this book has explored a broad range of parallels between *Star Wars* and the Vedic tradition. Let's briefly recap these parallels before delving into part II.

RECAP OF PART I

Chapter 1 discussed how Eastern philosophical traditions influenced *Star Wars*, as evidenced by the following quote by George Lucas: "The 'Force of others' [the precursor to the Force] is what all basic religions are based on, *especially the Eastern religions*, which is, essentially, that there is a force, God, whatever you want to call it."[24] Lucas was exposed to Eastern philosophy in several ways: (1) through producer Gary Kurtz, who had studied this subject; (2) through New Age spirituality, which draws heavily on Eastern ideas; and (3) through the Transcendental Meditation technique and the principles behind it.

Chapters 2–10 explored parallels between *Star Wars* and Eastern teachings—specifically, the Vedic teachings of ancient India.

Chapter 2 focused on the similarities between the Force and *Brahman*, meaning the pure consciousness that underlies and permeates the universe. Both are (1) associated with energy, (2) all-pervading, and (3) beyond the reach of the physical senses. Luke Skywalker learns to transcend the senses to use the Force, just as meditators transcend the senses to experience the state of pure consciousness. Using the Force is akin to enlivening the infinite intelligence of *Brahman*.

Chapter 2 also mentioned the "supernatural" abilities exhibited by the Jedi and (allegedly) the ancient *siddhas*, which include knowledge of the future, levitation, mastery over the elements, and out-of-body travel. The Jedi and the *siddhas* cultivated these abilities through practices like meditation and yoga.

Chapter 3 compared the light side of the Force to *sattva*, the Vedic force of creation; it likened the dark side to *tamas*, the Vedic force of destruction. This chapter observed that *Star Wars* and the Vedic tradition warn against anger, fear, and aggression.

Chapter 4 discussed how—in both *Star Wars* and Vedic teachings—there is a natural balance between light/creation and darkness/destruction. However, sometimes this state of equilibrium is lost, resulting in widespread suffering. In the Vedic tradition, *dharma* is the power of nature that maintains balance; when this power becomes weakened, imbalance occurs. In *Star Wars*, imbalance happens when the Sith overshadow the Jedi.

Chapter 4 also considered the parallels between the *Star Wars* heroes and the Vedic avatars (direct incarnations of pure consciousness). These heroes and avatars (1) restore balance, (2) protect the righteous, and (3) destroy the wicked.

In addition, chapter 4 pointed out that both the Force and *dharma* bind the universe together. It discussed personal *dharma*, meaning the path of evolution that is tailored to an individual. This chapter highlighted the following principles: (1) personal *dharma* is connected to one's innate tendencies; (2) by following one's *dharma*, one may reach their full potential; and (3) everyone has a *dharmic* role to play in this world. From a Vedic perspective, it is Luke's *dharma* to become a Jedi Knight and Rebel fighter.

Chapter 5 explored how both *Star Wars* and the Vedic tradition support the idea that "we are all connected." From a Vedic standpoint, this interconnectedness makes it possible for our thoughts to affect other people. In *Star Wars*, this interconnectedness allows the Jedi and the Sith to sense one another's presence, feelings, and intentions, even from far away.

Furthermore, chapter 5 discussed the Vedic principle of collective consciousness, meaning the combined awareness of all the individuals in a group. Collective consciousness can be either *sattvic* (pure and creative) or *tamasic* (dark and destructive). *Star Wars* depicts both positive and negative types of combined awareness. These themes are evident in the climax of *The Rise of Skywalker*, in which Rey embodies all the Jedi and Emperor Palpatine embodies all the Sith.

Chapter 6 noted that *Star Wars* and the Vedic texts express an optimistic view of death; they portray dying as a natural process not to be feared. Both sources contain the principle of immortality, which takes one of two forms: either (1) the immortality of the individual spirit or (2) the immortality of union with the Force/*Brahman*.

Chapter 7 pointed out that "there is no such thing as luck"[25] in *Star Wars* or the Vedic tradition. From a Vedic perspective, this concept is based on the principles that (1) life is purposeful and (2) karma will eventually play out. These principles seem applicable to *Star Wars*, which indicates that good will triumph over evil in the end.

Chapter 7 also discussed right and wrong. It noted that both the Jedi and Vedic teachers see a calm, peaceful state of awareness as the ideal basis for virtuous action.

Chapter 8 explored the topics of intuition and non-attachment. Both *Star Wars* and the Vedic tradition depict the power of intuition. They refer to an all-pervading reality that underlies this mental faculty—namely, the Force/*Brahman*. Furthermore, these sources value non-attachment, encouraging us to let go of our individual limitations.

Chapter 9 noted that the *Star Wars* concepts of strong-mindedness and weak-mindedness have parallels in the Vedic tradition. It also discussed knowledge, pointing out that the Jedi and Vedic teachers share the following views: (1) knowledge is immensely valuable; (2) it can be gained from within; (3) it should be supplemented by experience; and (4) the opposite of knowledge—ignorance—must be overcome.

Chapter 10 (this chapter) began by asking, "What are we fundamentally?" It noted that according to *Star Wars* and Vedic teachings, our true nature is nonphysical. This chapter also pointed out that the Jedi and Vedic teachers value selflessness and positivity. Lastly, it discussed redemption, a theme that is found in both *Star Wars* and the Vedic tradition.

Now that we've explored these parallels, let's turn to part II: "Universal Truths in *Star Wars*."

Part II

UNIVERSAL TRUTHS IN *STAR WARS*

Chapter 11

THE BLIND MEN AND THE ELEPHANT

In the Indian parable of the blind men and the elephant, several sightless individuals want to know what an elephant is like. They find one, and each man touches a different part of it. One touches its trunk and states that the elephant is like a snake—long, narrow, and flexible. Another touches its leg and asserts that this animal is like a tree—strong and sturdy. Another touches its ear and remarks that the elephant is like a fan—wide and flat. The last person touches its tail and declares that this animal is like a rope—thin and cordlike. Each man correctly describes one part of the elephant but incorrectly concludes that his description encapsulates the entire animal.

This parable has been applied to different religions. Each religion is like one of the blind men, accurately perceiving certain aspects of life but not seeing the whole picture.

George Lucas referred to this analogy in a 1999 interview with American journalist Bill Moyers (born in 1934). To quote one of Lucas's statements from this interview, "All the religions are true, they just see a different part of the elephant."[1]

We might say that the elephant symbolizes "the essence of all religions," meaning the ultimate truth beyond religious differences. Recall the following quote by Lucas:

> The Force evolved out of various developments of character and plot. I wanted a concept of religion based on the premise that there is a God and there is good and evil. I began to distill *the essence of all religions* into what I thought was a basic idea common to all religions and common to primitive thinking. I wanted to develop something that was nondenominational but still had a kind of religious reality. I believe in God

and I believe in right and wrong. I also believe that there are basic tenets which through history have developed into certainties, such as "thou shalt not kill." I don't want to hurt other people. "Do unto others . . ." is the philosophy that permeates my work.[2]

Given Lucas's perspective on these topics, it is no surprise that the *Star Wars* films contain parallels to the religions and philosophies of the world. These films seem to embody universal truths (i.e., they give us a glimpse of the whole elephant rather than focusing exclusively on one part).

Note: This book does not provide a comprehensive list of the similarities between *Star Wars* and religious/philosophical traditions. It is more of a sampler platter, allowing readers to "taste" these similarities in bite-sized portions.

THE ALL-PERVADING FORCE

The Force corresponds with principles from many religious/philosophical traditions beyond the Vedic tradition. It is similar to the Great Spirit described in various Native American and First Nations cultures. The Penobscot tribesman Bedagi, aka Big Thunder (1827–1906), refers to the omnipresence of this Supreme Being: "The Great Spirit is in all things; he is in the air we breathe."[3] The same statement applies to the Force, which is "in all things," including the air.

The Force is also analogous to the Tao, the central principle of Taoism (an ancient Chinese religious/philosophical tradition). To quote the most influential Taoist text, the Tao Te Ching, "The great Tao flows unobstructed in every direction."[4] Thus, the Tao flows everywhere; like the Force, it is all-pervading. In addition, the Tao is beyond the physical senses: "Look for it, and it can't be seen. / Listen for it, and it can't be heard. / Grasp for it, and it can't be caught."[5] These statements apply to the Force, which cannot be seen, heard, or touched.

Lucas has likened the Force to God: "The 'Force of others' [the precursor to the Force] is what all basic religions are based on . . . which is, essentially, that there is a force, God, whatever you want to call it."[6]

Even the Bible includes verses about God that are reminiscent of the Force. To quote the Book of Psalms, a text found in both Jewish and Christian scripture, "Where can I go from your Spirit? Where can I flee from your presence? If I go up to the heavens, you are there; if I make my bed in the depths, you are there" (Pss. 139:7–8 NIV). According to this verse, the Spirit of God, like the Force, is in all places.

The following passage from the Christian New Testament also recalls the Force: "The God who made the world and everything in it is the Lord of heaven and earth and does not live in temples built by human hands" (Acts 17:24 NIV). In other words, God's presence is not restricted to religious sites. Indeed, "he is not far from any one of us. 'For in him we live and move and have our being'" (Acts 17:27–28 NIV). One could apply these principles to *Star Wars* by stating that in the Force, the Jedi live and move and have their being.

Another verse from the New Testament dovetails with the concept of the Force: "He [Jesus Christ] is before all things, and in Him all things hold together" (Col. 1:17 NIV). This verse parallels Luke Skywalker's statement that the Force "binds the universe together."[7]

Some Muslim quotes align with the idea of the Force. For instance, take the following statement by the influential Islamic philosopher Ibn Arabi (1165–1240): "God, the omnipresent and omniscient, cannot be confined to any one creed. For he says [in the Quran]: 'Wheresoever ye turn, there is the face of Allah.'"[8] One could apply these principles to *Star Wars* by stating that wherever you turn, there is the Force.

The following passage from the Granth Sahib, the central scripture of Sikhism,[9] also corresponds with the concept of the Force:

> Chant, and meditate on the One God, who permeates and pervades the many beings of the whole Universe. God created it, and God spreads through it everywhere. Everywhere I look, I see God. The Perfect Lord is perfectly pervading and permeating the water, the land and the sky; there is no place without Him.[10]

Similarly, we could say that the Force "is perfectly pervading and permeating the water, the land and the sky; there is no place without" it.

In summary, the Force correlates with religious/philosophical concepts from around the world; therefore, we might call it a universal principle.

THE FORCE WITHIN

In *The Last Jedi*, Rey observes that the Force is within herself.[11] This principle coincides with the Vedic tradition, which teaches that *Brahman* is within every human being.

Many religious/philosophical traditions contain similar concepts. For example, from the perspective of various Native American and First Nations cultures, the Great Spirit is within each of us. To quote Black Elk (1863–1950), a Lakota medicine man:

> The first peace, which is the most important, is that which comes within the souls of men when they realize their relationship, their oneness, with the universe and all its Powers, and when they realize that at the center of the universe dwells Wakan-Tanka [the Great Spirit], and that this center is really everywhere, it is within each of us.[12]

Likewise, the Force "is really everywhere, it is within each of us."

This principle recalls the Tao Te Ching, which refers to "the Tao inside you."[13] Just as Taoists perceive the Tao within themselves, so Rey observes the Force within herself.

The Christian New Testament includes an analogous idea, describing the kingdom of God as being within us. To quote the Gospel of Luke:

> Now when He [Jesus] was asked by the Pharisees when the kingdom of God would come, He answered them and said, "The kingdom of God does not come with observation; nor will they say, 'See here!' or 'See there!'" For indeed, *the kingdom of God is within you.* (Luke 17:20–21 NKJV)[14]

The First Epistle to the Corinthians expresses a similar concept: "Do you not know that you are the temple of God and *that* the Spirit of God dwells in you?" (1 Cor. 3:16 NKJV). According to these verses, the kingdom/Spirit of God is not a separate entity; rather, like the Force, it dwells within us.

In the Islamic tradition, the Sufis (mystics) have voiced the same basic idea. To quote the Sufi leader Bawa Muhaiyaddeen (died in 1986), "So then where is the kingdom of God in man? It is in the heart. That is heaven. That is God."[15] In short, God, like the Force, is within every person.

Similarly, the famous Sufi poet Rumi (1207–1273) states, "There is a life-force within your soul, seek that life. There is a gem in the mountain of your body, seek that mine."[16] We see that the "life-force," like Lucas's Force, can be found within.

We find a parallel concept in the Granth Sahib, the primary text of Sikhism. Here are three relevant quotes from this text: (1) "The Lord dwells within you." (2) "One who understands himself finds the Mansion of the Lord's Presence within his own home. Imbued with the True Lord, Truth is gathered in." (3) "My Father [God] has revealed Himself within me."[17] Each of these quotes expresses the same essential idea: the Lord is within. Likewise, in *Star Wars*, the Force is within.

In conclusion, Rey's observation that the Force exists within herself corresponds with principles from many religious/philosophical traditions.

"MAY THE FORCE BE WITH YOU"

As any *Star Wars* fan knows, the Jedi often say to one another, "May the Force be with you." Essentially, this statement seems to mean "May the Force support your endeavors." We see an example of such support in *A New Hope* when Luke uses the Force to destroy the Death Star.

The phrase "May the Force be with you" has parallels in many religious/philosophical traditions (including the Vedic tradition). Just as the Jedi desire support from the Force, so the followers of many religions and philosophies desire support from something greater than themselves. For instance, various Native American and First Nations cultures look to the Great Spirit for support, as illustrated by the three following quotes.

> From a Sioux prayer translated by the late nineteenth-century chief Yellow Lark: "Oh Great Spirit, Whose voice I hear in the winds, and whose breath gives life to all the world, hear me. I am a man before You, one of Your many children—I am small and weak. I need your strength and wisdom."[18] Thus, the Sioux seek strength and wisdom from the Great Spirit, just as the Jedi seek strength and knowledge from the Force.
>
> From a Mi'kmaq prayer expressed by leader Noel Knockwood (1932–2014): "O Great Spirit, who art before all else and who dwells in every object, in every person and in every place, we cry unto thee, we summon thee from the far places into our present awareness."[19] This prayer suggests that the Mi'kmaq people attempt to connect with the Great Spirit, like the Jedi who feel the Force around them.
>
> From a Cherokee prayer: "May the Great Spirit, Bless all who enter there."[20] The Jedi version of this quote might run as follows: "May the Force be with all who enter there."

In each case, receiving the blessing of the Great Spirit is akin to receiving support from the Force.

Jews and Christians also seek assistance from something greater than themselves—God. Many biblical statements express this theme, including the phrase "May the Lord be with you." Most commentators agree that this phrase probably inspired the *Star Wars* line "May the Force be with you."

Like Jews and Christians, Muslims request help from God. It is easiest to see the parallels between Muslim prayers and *Star Wars* concepts when we consult the writings of the Sufis (mystics). For example, one Universal Sufi prayer starts with the following line: "Praise be to Thee, Most Supreme God, / Omnipotent, Omnipresent, All-Pervading, The Only Being."[21] After this line, the prayer asks for blessings from God. These sentiments recall the Jedi, who desire the support of the all-pervading Force.

In addition, Sikhs seek assistance from God. Their traditional morning prayer begins with the following words: "There is One God. / He is the supreme truth. / He, The Creator, / Is without fear and without hate. / He, The Omnipresent, / Pervades the universe."[22] Thus, as previously noted, the Sikh God is all-pervading like the Force. In other prayers, Sikhs request specific blessings, which is analogous to using the Force to achieve particular outcomes.

In summary, both the Jedi and the followers of various religious/ philosophical traditions desire support from something greater than themselves, whether that be the Force, God, or the Great Spirit. So, we could say, "May the Force be with you," "May the Lord be with you," or "May the Great Spirit be with you"; in the right context, each of these sayings would make sense.

SUPERNATURAL ABILITIES

The Jedi's "supernatural" abilities include lifting objects via their minds, foreseeing the future, levitating, and projecting their awareness to other places. The Vedic tradition also describes these abilities, as do other religious/philosophical traditions, such as Buddhism.

Although Buddhists do not believe in an all-pervading force or god, their sacred texts do refer to the attainment of supernatural powers through meditation. These powers include (1) "the ability to go anywhere at will and to transform oneself or objects at will," (2) "'the divine eyes' capable of seeing anything at any distance and the future destiny of oneself and others," (3) "'the divine ears' capable of hearing any sound at any distance," (4) "the ability to know others' mind and thoughts," (5) "the ability to know former lives of oneself and others," and (6) "the ability to destroy all evil passions."[23] Of these, the ability to foresee the future (see the "Mind-to-Mind Effects: 'The Force Is Strong with This One!'" section in chapter 5) and the ability to know the minds and thoughts of others (see the "Strong-Mindedness and Weak-Mindedness" section in chapter 9) are most reminiscent of the Jedi.

Note that the Buddha warned against seeking supernatural powers for their own sake. He taught that the goal of life is to attain *nirvana* (enlightenment), not flashy abilities.[24]

Like Buddhism, Taoism refers to supernatural powers. For instance, in Taoist literature, the ancient philosopher Liezi (Lieh Tzu) possessed such powers. To quote the Zhuangzi, one of the primary Taoist texts, "Liezi could ride the wind and go soaring around with cool and breezy skill."[25]

Liezi has been credited with composing a Taoist text of his own, which was named after him. This text also mentions supernatural abilities:

> The man of perfect faith can extend his influence to inanimate things and disembodied spirits; he can move heaven and earth, and fly to the six cardinal points without encountering any hindrance. . . . His powers are not confined to walking in perilous places and passing through water and fire.[26]

These abilities recall the Jedi. Although they can't fly, they can levitate and project their awareness to other locations. They can also "influence . . . inanimate objects" by using the Force to summon, lift, or throw them.

Various Native American and First Nations cultures refer to miraculous abilities, too, which they attribute to medicine men/women. These individuals are thought to be able to heal the sick, influence the weather, and even foresee the future. Sarah Winnemucca (1844–1891), a Northern Paiute author, describes the role of a medicine man in her tribe:

> He is supposed to be in communion with spirits. . . . He cures the sick by laying on of hands, and prayers and incantations and heavenly songs. He infuses new life into the patient, and performs most wonderful feats of skill in his practice.[27]

The Oglala Sioux chief Flat-Iron (Maza Blaska) discusses the source of the medicine man's abilities: "From Wakan Tanka, the Great Mystery, comes all power. It is from Wakan Tanka that the holy man has wisdom and the power to heal and to make holy charms."[28]

These concepts are reminiscent of the Jedi, who can foresee the future and heal other people or creatures (as Rey does in *The Rise of Skywalker*).

These abilities come from the Force, which is analogous to Wakan Tanka, the Great Spirit.

Like the religious/philosophical traditions discussed thus far, Judaism contains stories of miraculous events. For instance, take the parting of the Red Sea recounted in the Hebrew Bible (also known as the Tanakh):

> Then [the prophet] Moses stretched out his hand over the sea, and all that night the Lord drove the sea back with a strong east wind and turned it into dry land. The waters were divided, and the Israelites went through the sea on dry ground, with a wall of water on their right and on their left. (Exod. 14:21–22 NIV)

The Hebrew Bible mentions numerous other miracles, including transfigurations, the curing of leprosy, and the resurrection of the dead. The prophets perform these wonders through the power of God. These individuals are like the Jedi, who achieve supernatural feats through the power of the Force.

The Christian New Testament also describes a wide array of miracles, which are performed by Jesus and his disciples (except for the Transfiguration, which happens to Jesus himself). These wonders include healings (of blindness, deafness, muteness, paralysis, leprosy, and other disabilities/ailments), the resurrection of the dead, and control over nature (turning water into wine, walking on water, calming the storm, etc.). Once again, these feats recall the Jedi, who can heal (as Rey does in *The Rise of Skywalker*) and control nature in various ways (for instance, by Force-lifting rocks).

The following statement by Jesus regarding miracles parallels Jedi teachings: "Truly I tell you, if you have faith as small as a mustard seed, you can say to this mountain, 'Move from here to there,' and it will move. Nothing will be impossible for you" (Matt. 17:20 NIV). The Jedi agree that nothing is impossible; General Leia Organa, who has received Jedi training, states this principle outright in *The Rise of Skywalker*. As for moving mountains, this feat may not happen in *Star Wars*, but Yoda does lift Luke's starship out of the swamp in *The Empire Strikes Back*.

Another biblical passage expresses a similar theme: "What is impossible with man is possible with God" (Luke 18:27 NIV). The Jedi version might run as follows: "What seems impossible is possible with the Force."

Like Judaism and Christianity, Islam refers to miracles, such as those (allegedly) performed by Moses and Jesus. Annemarie Schimmel, former professor of Indo-Muslim Culture at Harvard University, comments on this topic: "[The prophet] Muhammad, whose only miracle according to his own words was the bringing of the Qur'ān, is credited with innumerable miracles and associated with a variety of miraculous occurrences."[29] The miracles attributed to Muhammad include healing by touch, predicting the future, and controlling nature in various ways. Yet again, these abilities recall the Jedi.

Since the Islamic Sufis (mystics) came up in previous sections, it is worth noting the following quote by the Sufi poet Rumi: "Never lose hope, my heart, miracles dwell in the invisible. If the whole world turns against you keep your eyes on the Friend."[30] Here, "the invisible" and "the Friend" seem to refer to the divine. The Jedi version of this quote might run as follows: "Never lose hope, because all things are possible through the invisible Force. If the whole world turns against you, stay connected to the Force, which is your ally."

Thus, many religious/philosophical traditions refer to supernatural powers and/or miracles, which are reminiscent of the Jedi's abilities.

MEDITATION AND INNER PEACE

The Jedi maintain their connection to the Force partially through meditation, a practice that is also found in the Vedic tradition. Many other religious/philosophical traditions contain some form of meditation, as illustrated by the following quotes.

From the Buddhist Dhammapada (the sayings of the Buddha): "He who gives himself to vanity, and does not give himself to meditation, forgetting the real aim (of life) and grasping at pleasure, will in time envy him who has exerted himself in meditation."[31] In other words, meditation is more rewarding than chasing after superficial pleasures. Certainly, the Jedi would agree with this perspective. (Note: Not all styles of meditation require exertion; some are automatic/effortless. For more on this topic, see appendix A.)

From the Taoist Tao Te Ching: "Those who know do not talk. / Those who talk do not know. / Stop talking, / meditate in silence."[32] According to this quote, we should stop theorizing about the truth and instead discover it firsthand through meditation. Likewise, according to the Jedi, we should do more than talk about the Force; we should also meditate to feel its presence.

From the Jewish rabbi Chaim Yosef David Azulai (1724–1806): "The root of everything is meditation (hitbodedut). It is a very great and lofty concept [practice], making a person worthy of all holiness.

. . . When a person meditates, he is clothed with holiness. . . . When one meditates, he is also attached to God, even with regard to his mundane bodily needs."[33] In short, through meditation, one becomes "attached to God." Similarly, through meditation, the Jedi become connected to the Force.

From the Christian priest and mystic St. John of the Cross (1542–1591): "Seek in reading and you will find in meditation; knock in prayer and it will be opened to you in contemplation."[34] This quote suggests that the reading of scripture is not sufficient for complete understanding; one needs to supplement this activity with meditation. This approach recalls the Jedi, who meditate in addition to reading sacred texts.

From Omar Edaibat, a Muslim volunteer at McGill University's Office of Religious and Spiritual Life: "The word often used for Islamic 'meditation' is '*dhikr*', meaning 'remembrance.' The goal of meditating and 'worship' (*ibada*) for Muslims is to remember God, the Sustainer, Creator, and Caretaker of all existence."[35] As Muslims meditate on the Lord, the Jedi meditate to feel the Force.

From the Sikh Granth Sahib: "Chant, and meditate on the One God, who permeates and pervades the many beings of the whole Universe."[36] Again, this quote is reminiscent of the Jedi, who meditate to connect with the all-pervading Force.

We see that there are notable similarities between Jedi meditation and meditation across religious/philosophical traditions.

To explore this subject further, consider the scene in *The Phantom Menace* in which Qui-Gon Jinn and Darth Maul are briefly separated in the middle of their duel. Qui-Gon uses this opportunity to meditate. While doing so, he appears calm, which suggests that he is experiencing some degree of inner peace.

This concept has parallels in the Vedic tradition, which teaches that the state of yoga is deeply peaceful.

Inner peace is an important theme in many other religious/philosophical traditions. In Buddhism, this quality is associated with spiritual maturity. To quote the Dhammapada, "Him I call indeed a Brahmana [a holy person] who is bright like the moon, pure, serene, undisturbed."[37] According to this quote, holy people are naturally serene. How to gain this state of tranquility? Through meditation.

Taoism also values inner peace. To quote the Tao Te Ching, "If you can empty your mind of all thoughts / your heart will embrace the tranquility of peace."[38] In other words, when the mind transcends thought during meditation, the heart becomes peaceful.

Likewise, various Native American and First Nations cultures encourage people to cultivate inner peace. To return to an earlier quote by the Lakota medicine man Black Elk:

> The first peace, which is the most important, is that which comes within the souls of men when they realize their relationship, their oneness, with the universe and all its Powers, and when they realize that at the center of the universe dwells Wakan-Tanka [the Great Spirit], and that this center is really everywhere, it is within each of us.[39]

Thus, we experience "the first peace" when we realize our connection to the universe and the omnipresent Great Spirit.

The topic of inner peace also comes up in Judaism, as illustrated by the following passage from the Hebrew Bible: "The Lord bless you and keep you; the Lord make his face shine on you and be gracious to you; the Lord turn his face toward you and give you peace" (Num. 6:24–26 NIV). This passage indicates that God bestows inner peace.

The Christian New Testament contains similar themes, as evidenced by the following verses. From the Gospel of John: "[Jesus said,] 'Peace I leave with you; my peace I give you. I do not give to you as the world gives. Do not let your hearts be troubled and do not be afraid'" (John 14:27 NIV). From the Epistle to the Philippians: "And the peace of God, which transcends all understanding, will guard your hearts and your minds in Christ Jesus" (Phil. 4:7 NIV). From the Second Epistle to the Thessalonians: "Now may the Lord of peace himself give you peace at all times and in every way. The Lord be with all you" (2 Thess. 3:16 NIV). These verses associate inner peace with God and/or Jesus Christ.

This discussion recalls a quote by the Christian theologian St. Augustine of Hippo (354–430): "[Lord,] you have made us for yourself, and our heart is restless until it rests in you."[40] This quote implies that inner peace comes through communion with God.

We find a parallel statement in the Koran: "Now surely by Allah's remembrance are the hearts set at rest."[41] In other words, when one remembers God, their heart finds rest. This point corresponds with another Koranic verse that refers to the Lord as "the Giver of peace."[42]

The same concept appears in the Granth Sahib, the central text of Sikhism: "The Lord Himself, the Life of the World, is the Giver of Peace."[43] This peace may be attained through meditation: "Those who meditate on You, Lord, those who meditate on You—those humble beings dwell in peace in this world."[44]

In conclusion, inner peace is an essential theme in many religious/ philosophical traditions. This theme dovetails with Qui-Gon's calm meditation in *The Phantom Menace.*

Chapter 12

OPPOSITES AND BALANCE

Our lives are an interplay of opposites. We perceive light in the morning and darkness at night. We perspire from the heat in the summer and shiver with cold in the winter. Even our mental states can rocket between extremes; we may feel joyful in one moment and gloomy in the next.

Opposites play an essential role in *Star Wars* (think of the light and dark sides of the Force) and many religious/philosophical traditions, including the Vedic tradition.

LIGHT, DARKNESS, AND OTHER OPPOSITES

Like *Star Wars*, Buddhism discusses the opposites of light and darkness. The Dhammapada describes wise individuals as "full of light."[1] It asks, "Why do you not seek a light, ye who are surrounded by darkness?"[2] In these quotes, darkness represents ignorance, and light symbolizes the truth.

In ancient Chinese philosophy, the primary opposites are *yin* and *yang*. *Yin* is associated with femininity, passivity, and darkness, whereas *yang* is associated with masculinity, activity, and light. It is said that the interaction between these two forces created the universe and everything in it.

In Judaism, the Hebrew Bible refers to the opposites of light and darkness. Sometimes these words are used literally, as in the following passage from the Book of Genesis: "And God said, 'Let there be light,' and there was light. God saw that the light was good, and he separated the light from the darkness" (Gen. 1:3–4 NIV). In other cases, "light" and "darkness" are used allegorically, as in this verse from the Book of Psalms: "Even in darkness light dawns for the upright, for those who are gracious and compassionate and righteous" (Ps. 112:4 NIV). Here, darkness seems to represent misfortune, whereas light appears to symbolize good fortune.

The Christian New Testament also discusses the opposites of light and darkness. To quote the Epistle to the Ephesians, "For you were once darkness, but now you are light in the Lord. Live as children of light (for the fruit of the light consists in all goodness, righteousness and truth)" (Eph. 5:8–9 NIV). This passage correlates light with "goodness, righteousness and truth," suggesting that darkness corresponds with evil and untruth. These principles seem consistent with the following verse from the Gospel of John: "The light shines in the darkness, and the darkness has not overcome it" (John 1:5 NIV). In other words, righteousness and truth shine in the face of evil and untruth.

The Koran discusses light and darkness as well. Like the Hebrew Bible, it sometimes uses these terms literally, as we see in the following excerpt: "All praise is due to Allah [God], Who created the heavens and the earth and made the darkness and the light."[3] In other cases, the Koran refers to light and darkness allegorically, as we observe in this verse: "With it Allah guides him who will follow His pleasure into the ways of safety and brings them out of utter darkness into light by His will and guides them to the right path."[4] Here, the move from darkness to light seems to symbolize the discovery of truth.

The primary text of Sikhism, the Granth Sahib, also contains the themes of light and darkness. It states, "The Guru [spiritual teacher] has applied the true ointment of spiritual wisdom to my eyes. Deep within, the Divine Light has dawned, and the darkness of ignorance has been dispelled."[5] Once again, light seems to represent the truth, whereas darkness signifies ignorance.

In summary, opposites play an essential role in *Star Wars* (think of the light and dark sides of the Force) and many religious/philosophical traditions (think of light and darkness, *yin* and *yang*, etc.).

What leads a person into spiritual darkness? Let's explore this topic next.

THE PATH TO DARKNESS

Chapter 3 listed three tendencies that can lead a Jedi into darkness: anger, fear, and aggression. The Vedic tradition also warns about these tendencies. So do other religious/philosophical traditions, as we will see in the following pages. Let's begin with the topic of anger.

In Buddhism, the Dhammapada warns the reader not to "yield to anger."[6] This ancient text states, "Him I call indeed a Brahmana [holy person] who is free from anger."[7] The following verse suggests how to escape from this emotion: "If, like a shattered metal plate (gong), thou utter not, then thou hast reached Nirvana; contention is not known to thee."[8] In other words, through meditation, the mind may become as silent as a broken gong; with regular practice, one may attain *nirvana* (enlightenment). In this state, anger and contention do not overshadow one's inner peace.

Like Buddhism, various Native American and First Nations cultures refer to the harmful effects of anger. To quote an Omaha proverb, "In anger a man becomes dangerous to himself and to others."[9] Similarly, a Hopi proverb states, "Do not allow anger to poison you."[10]

The Hebrew Bible also cautions the reader against unchecked anger. To quote the Book of Psalms, "Refrain from anger and turn from wrath; do not fret—it leads only to evil" (Ps. 37:8 NIV). Likewise, the Book of Proverbs states, "Whoever is patient has great understanding, but one who is quick-tempered displays folly" (Prov. 14:29 NIV); stated another way, one who is quick to anger lacks good judgment.

The Christian New Testament contains parallel themes. For instance, consider the following verse from the Epistle to the Ephesians: "Get rid of all bitterness, rage and anger, brawling and slander, along with every form of malice" (Eph. 4:31 NIV). For another example, take this passage from the Epistle of James: "Everyone should be quick to listen, slow to speak and slow to become angry, because human anger does not produce the righteousness that God desires" (James 1:19–20 NIV).

The Koran and the *hadith* (a record of the words and actions of the prophet Muhammad) express analogous ideas. According to the Koran, God loves "those who restrain (their) anger and pardon men."[11] The *hadith* offers practical advice for subduing anger: "If one of you is angry while he is standing, let him sit down so his anger will leave him; otherwise, let him lie down."[12]

In Sikhism, the Granth Sahib describes the detrimental effects of anger: "The heart is filled with anger and violence, which cause all sense to be forgotten."[13] This text urges the reader to overcome anger by meditating on the name of the Lord (a core Sikh practice).

We see that many religious/philosophical traditions advise us to refrain from anger—the first tendency that can lead a Jedi into darkness.

What about the second tendency: fear?

Buddhism encourages us to transcend this tendency by meditating and thereby cultivating a state of inner peace. In this state, there is no room for fear. To quote the Dhammapada, "He who has tasted the sweetness of solitude and tranquillity [*sic*], is free from fear."[14]

Taoism indicates that we can overcome fear by following the way of the Tao (i.e., by living in harmony with the universe). The Tao Te Ching states, "She who follows the way of the Tao / will draw the world to her steps. / She can go without fear of being injured, / because she has found peace and tranquility in her heart."[15]

Judaism urges its followers to conquer fear through faith in God. To quote the Book of Isaiah, "So do not fear, for I am with you; do not be dismayed, for I am your God. I will strengthen you and help you; I will uphold you with my righteous right hand" (Isa. 41:10 NIV). According to this verse, the Jewish people need not be afraid because they will receive assistance from the divine. The Book of Psalms contains parallel verses, such as the following: "Even though I walk through the darkest valley, I will fear no evil, for you [God] are with me" (Ps. 23:4 NIV). This verse indicates that the presence of the Lord can dispel fear.

The Christian New Testament also encourages fearlessness. To quote the Gospel of John, "[Jesus said,] 'Peace I leave with you; my peace I give you. I do not give to you as the world gives. Do not let your hearts be troubled and do not be afraid'" (John 14:27 NIV). This verse suggests that faith in Jesus Christ can bring inner peace, which in turn can eliminate fear. Here is another relevant verse, which comes from the Second Epistle to Timothy: "For the Spirit God gave us does not make us timid, but gives us power, love and self-discipline" (2 Tim. 1:7 NIV). According to this verse, the Holy Spirit within every Christian imbues them with positive qualities, not timidity.

Similarly, the Koran teaches that devout and honorable Muslims have no reason to fear: "Yes! Whoever submits himself entirely to Allah and he is the doer of good (to others) he has his reward from his Lord, and there is no fear for him nor shall he grieve."[16]

The Sikh Granth Sahib urges us to transcend fear through meditation: "Those who meditate on the Fearless One, on the Fearless Lord—all their fears are dispelled."[17] This quote suggests that meditators can embody the qualities of the divine, such as fearlessness.

In addition, various Native American and First Nations leaders prompted their followers to conquer their fear. For instance, take the following statement by Chief Tecumseh (1768–1813) of the Shawnee tribe: "Live your life that the fear of death can never enter your heart."[18]

Thus, many religions and philosophies encourage their adherents to overcome fear—which is the second tendency that can lead a Jedi into darkness.

What about the third tendency: aggression? Do religious/philosophical traditions condemn this quality? This is a difficult question to answer. Many religious texts encourage peacefulness, but some seem to condone violence. Furthermore, many people of faith act harmoniously, while others attempt to suppress opposing views.

Whenever a religious individual or group commits an act of aggression, it is worth asking whether that act is in the true spirit of their belief system. For instance, if a Buddhist were to attack someone without provocation, this action would go against the Buddhist doctrine of *ahimsa*, which means "noninjury." Thus, we would not consider this attack representative of Buddhism itself.

It is not the goal of this book to rate the peacefulness or aggressiveness of different religious/philosophical traditions. Nor do I wish to analyze the seemingly violent passages in certain scriptures. I only want to share some relevant quotes that align with Jedi teachings, such as the following.

> From the Buddhist Dhammapada: "All men tremble at punishment, all men fear death; remember that you are like unto them, and do not kill, nor cause slaughter," and "All men tremble at punishment, all men love life; remember that thou art like unto them, and do not kill, nor cause slaughter."[19] Although the Jedi do engage in battle, they agree that we should avoid unnecessary violence.
>
> From the Taoist Tao Te Ching: "The one who overcomes an enemy should not dominate them."[20] "The skillful commander / strikes a decisive blow then stops."[21] "The best warriors / do not use violence. / The best generals / do not destroy indiscriminately. / The best tacticians / try to avoid confrontation."[22] The Jedi would approve of this moderate approach to warfare.
>
> From Cornplanter (1732–1836), a Seneca chief: "It is my wish and the wishes of my people to live peaceably and quietly with you and yours."[23] The Jedi also desire peace.
>
> From the Hebrew Bible: "Better a patient person than a warrior, one with self-control than one who takes a city" (Prov. 16:32 NIV). The Jedi, too, praise patience and self-control.
>
> From the Christian New Testament: "Blessed are the merciful, for they will be shown mercy" (Matt. 5:7 NIV); "Blessed are the peacemakers, for they will be called children of God" (Matt. 5:9 NIV); "But I

tell you, love your enemies and pray for those who persecute you" (Matt. 5:44 NIV). The Jedi also value mercy, peace, and compassion.

From the Muslim Koran: "And fight in the way of Allah with those who fight with you, and do not exceed the limits, surely Allah does not love those who exceed the limits."[24] To "exceed the limits" means to commit atrocities such as killing old men, women, and children.[25] Certainly, the Jedi strive never to commit atrocities.

From the Sikh Granth Sahib: "Now, the Merciful Lord has issued His Command. Let no one chase after and attack anyone else. Let all abide in peace, under this Benevolent Rule."[26] Likewise, the Jedi discourage unprovoked attacks.

We see that these religious/philosophical quotes encourage peacefulness and discourage aggression—the third tendency that can lead a Jedi into darkness.

In summary, many religious/philosophical traditions view anger and fear in a negative light; furthermore, some of these traditions, such as Buddhism, look down on aggression. The Jedi have similar perspectives on these issues.

Now that we've talked about light and darkness, as well as the tendencies that lead to darkness, let's consider the value of balance.

BALANCE

Chapter 4 discussed the importance of balance between the light and dark sides of the Force. It noted that the Vedic tradition contains parallel concepts.

Many other religious/philosophical traditions also value balance. In Buddhism, this quality is associated with following "a middle way . . . between the extremes of asceticism and sensual indulgence."[27] From a Buddhist perspective, it is best to avoid both rigid self-denial and unrestrained self-gratification.

Likewise, balance is an essential theme in Taoism. To quote the Tao Te Ching:

> The Tao of Heaven works in the world
> like the drawing of a bow.
> The top is bent downward;
> the bottom is bent up.
> The excess is taken from,

and the deficient is given to.
The Tao works to use the excess,
and gives to that which is depleted.[28]

In other words, the Tao tends to balance out extremes. For example, in a room-temperature environment, it will cause hot water to cool down and ice cubes to melt.[29]

Furthermore, Taoism refers to the balance between *yin* (the feminine principle) and *yang* (the masculine principle). To quote the Tao Te Ching again, "All things carry Yin / yet embrace Yang. / They blend their life breaths / in order to produce harmony."[30] Simply stated, when *yin* and *yang* are integrated, there is harmony.

Various Native American and First Nations cultures also place importance on balance. Consider the following prayer from the Lakota tribe:

> Wakan Tanka, Great Mystery, teach me how to trust my heart, my mind, my intuition, my inner knowing, the senses of my body, the blessings of my spirit. Teach me to trust these things so that I may enter my Sacred Space and love beyond my fear, and thus Walk in Balance with the passing of each glorious Sun.[31]

According to this prayer, to "Walk in Balance," we must trust different aspects of ourselves, including our senses, mind, heart, intuition, and spirit.

In the Hebrew Bible—a text shared by Judaism and Christianity—various passages express the value of balance. For instance, take the following excerpt from the Book of Ecclesiastes:

> There is a time for everything,
> and a season for every activity under the heavens:
> a time to be born and a time to die,
> a time to plant and a time to uproot,
> a time to kill and a time to heal,
> a time to tear down and a time to build,
> a time to weep and a time to laugh,
> a time to mourn and a time to dance. (Eccles. 3:1–4 NIV)

The list continues, elaborating on the theme that there is a time for everything. This passage suggests that life should be a balance between the opposites of birth and death, tearing down and building up, weeping and laughing, and so on.

In the Koran, certain verses praise moderation, which is associated with balance. For example, take the following verse: "And thus We have made you a medium (just) nation that you may be the bearers of witness to the people."[32] Here, the Arabic word translated as "medium" or "just"—*wasat*— also means "moderate, balanced, and outstanding."[33] This verse suggests that Muslims should strive to embody the qualities just mentioned.

The Sikh Granth Sahib also refers to the value of balance: "O mind, dwell in the balanced state of your own inner being."[34] According to Sikhism, this state of consciousness can be gained through meditation. Here is another relevant quote from the same text: "The Gurmukhs dwell forever in balanced restraint."[35] (*Gurmukh* means one who is God-centered.[36])

Thus, many religious/philosophical traditions place importance on balance. So do the Jedi, as illustrated by their attempts to maintain equilibrium between the light and dark sides of the Force.

Chapter 13

DEATH, IMMORTALITY, AND PURPOSE

William Penn (1644–1718), founder of the colony of Pennsylvania, once wrote, "Life is eternal and love is immortal, and death is only an horizon, and an horizon is nothing save the limit of our sight."[1] According to this statement, death is not the ultimate end; it is only "the limit of our sight," which we cannot see past in this life. On the other side of death, life and love persist.

In *Star Wars*, the Jedi agree that death is not the ultimate end. So do many religious/philosophical traditions, as we will see later in this chapter. First, let's consider some relevant quotes about death.

PERSPECTIVES ON DEATH

Chapter 6 discussed the Jedi view that death is inevitable, like the coming of night. To quote Yoda's words from *Return of the Jedi*, "Twilight is upon me, and soon night must fall. That is the way of things . . . the way of the Force."[2] As previously noted, this concept has Vedic parallels.

Many other religious/philosophical traditions also emphasize the inevitability of death. For instance, take the following statement from the Buddhist Dhammapada: "The brilliant chariots of kings are destroyed, the body also approaches destruction."[3] In other words, the body is like a chariot or any other manufactured object—it will eventually deteriorate.

Likewise, Taoism refers to the inevitability of death. Here is a Taoist perspective expressed by scholar Bernard Down: "Death is like the progression of the four seasons, a natural part of the ebb and flow of transformations which constitute the movement of the Dao [aka the Tao]."⁴ Thus, a Taoist would agree with Yoda that "death is a natural part of life."⁵

We find the same theme in various Native American and First Nations cultures. To quote a proverb from the Blackfoot tribe, "Life is not independent from death—it only appears that way."⁶ In other words, life and death are interrelated, like two sides of the same coin. If this idea is true, then perhaps we don't need to fear our demise. That was the view of Chief Tecumseh of the Shawnee tribe, who urged people to "live your life that the fear of death can never enter your heart."⁷ He encouraged others to "prepare a noble death song for the day when you go over the great divide."⁸ Based on these quotes, it seems that we should not obsess over avoiding death; instead, we should focus on living—and eventually dying—well.

Like the religious/philosophical traditions just mentioned, Judaism refers to the inevitability of death. To quote the Book of Ecclesiastes, "Death is the destiny of everyone; the living should take this to heart" (Eccles. 7:2 NIV). This verse may inspire us to spend our time wisely.

Christianity also discusses the death of the body. The Apostle Paul writes on this topic in his Epistle to the Romans: "Who will rescue me from this body that is subject to death?" (Rom. 7:24 NIV). In this verse, he recognizes his mortality.

Similarly, Islam refers to the inevitability of death. According to the Koran, "Every soul shall taste of [i.e., experience] death."⁹ Furthermore, every person will die at an appointed time, regardless of their efforts to delay or hasten this event.¹⁰

Sikhism also portrays death as inevitable. To quote the Granth Sahib, "Life and death come to all who are born. Everything here gets devoured by Death. . . . Those who weep and wail might just as well all tie bundles of straw."¹¹ This passage suggests that it is pointless to "weep and wail" about something unavoidable.

In summary, many religious/philosophical traditions discuss the inevitability of death. This theme is also found in *Star Wars*, especially in the following quote by Yoda: "Twilight is upon me, and soon night must fall. That is the way of things . . . the way of the Force."¹²

Of course, in *Star Wars*, death is not the ultimate end. We find the same principle in various religious/philosophical traditions.

IMMORTALITY

Chapter 6 also discussed how there are essentially two types of immortality in *Star Wars*: (1) immortality through union with the Force, which is the fate of all people, and (2) individual immortality, which the Jedi learn to attain.

Many religious/philosophical traditions, including the Vedic tradition, also refer to immortality. Let's consider some examples.

Like *Star Wars*, Taoism describes different types of immortality. One type may be summarized as follows: "Man may die indeed, but his essence as part of the universal essence lives on forever."[13] In other words, our true essence will never perish. Another type is individual immortality, which can allegedly be gained through spiritual practices; one who achieves this goal is called a *xian*.[14]

Judaism also includes the concept of immortality. According to this religion, "humans have a soul which will one day return to God."[15] The exact nature of the afterlife, however, has been debated for centuries.

In the Christian New Testament, there are many references to immortality. Here are two quotes by Jesus on this topic: (1) "Do not be afraid of those who kill the body but cannot kill the soul" (Matt. 10:28 NIV); (2) "I give them [my followers] eternal life, and they shall never perish" (John 10:28 NIV). In this context, eternal life is associated with heaven.

The Koran also discusses immortality, referring to "the gardens of paradise" that the faithful will enter after death.[16] To quote this text, "And convey good news to those who believe and do good deeds, that they shall have gardens in which rivers flow."[17] These gardens are described as "abiding,"[18] which reveals their eternal nature.

In Islam, the Sufis (mystics) refer to immortality as well. To quote the Sufi poet Rumi, "Everyone is so afraid of death, but the real Sufis just laugh: nothing tyrannizes their hearts. What strikes the oyster shell does not damage the pearl."[19] It seems that the oyster shell symbolizes the body, whereas the pearl represents the soul. Thus, we might reword the poet's statement as follows: "What destroys the body does not damage the soul." Rumi further comments, "Our death is our wedding with eternity."[20] This statement suggests that when we die, we become one with the divine.

The Sikh Granth Sahib also discusses immortality: "Meditating on the True Lord, the status of immortality is obtained."[21] That is to say, through meditation the individual merges with God and thereby becomes eternal.

In addition, various Native American and First Nations cultures include the concept of immortality. To quote Christine Leigh Heyrman, professor of history at the University of Delaware, "The members of most tribes believed in the immortality of the human soul and an afterlife, the main feature of which was the abundance of every good thing that made earthly life secure and pleasant."[22]

In summary, both *Star Wars* and various religious/philosophical traditions contain the principle of immortality; they do not portray death as the ultimate end.

Of course, even if we are immortal, we can't devote all our attention to this topic. Instead, we need to decide how to spend our time in this life. With this goal in mind, it is helpful to ask questions such as "What is the purpose of life?" (if there is any purpose). Let's discuss this subject in relation to *Star Wars* and the religions and philosophies of the world.

PURPOSE

Chapter 7 mentioned the following *Star Wars* quote: "There is no such thing as luck."[23] This statement implies that nothing occurs by chance, which means that everything happens for a reason—life is inherently purposeful, not random or accidental. The same principles are found in the Vedic tradition.

Many other religious/philosophical traditions also refer to the purposefulness of life, as we will see in this section.

According to Buddhism, the purpose of life is to gain *nirvana* (enlightenment). To quote the Dhammapada, "These wise people, meditative, steady . . . attain to Nirvana, the highest happiness."[24] In this serene state, one is free from ignorance, fear, and suffering.

From a Taoist perspective, the purpose of life is to cultivate inner peace[25] and live in "harmony with the natural, balanced order of the universe."[26] The Tao Te Ching discusses the inner peace that can be gained through meditation and other spiritual practices: "If you can empty your mind of all thoughts / your heart will embrace the tranquility of peace."[27] The same text describes the life of a Taoist master who lives in harmony with the universe: "The Master accepts things as they are, and out of compassion avoids extravagance, excess and the extremes."[28]

Various Native American and First Nations cultures also refer to the purposefulness of life. To quote the Native American author Mourning Dove (1884–1936), "Everything on the earth has a purpose, every disease an herb to cure it, and every person a mission. This is the Indian theory of existence."[29] In other words, everything exists for a reason, and every person has a role to play in this world.

According to Judaism and Christianity, the purpose of life is to fulfill God's will. These religions teach that the Lord is all-knowing and guiding the world in a positive direction. Here are a couple biblical quotes regarding God's plans for His creation: from the Book of Psalms, "But the plans of the Lord stand firm forever, the purposes of his heart through all generations" (Ps. 33:11 NIV); from the Book of Jeremiah, "'For I know the plans I have for you,' declares the Lord, 'plans to prosper you and not to harm you, plans to give you hope and a future'" (Jer. 29:11 NIV). The goal, then, is to discover God's plan for one's life and align oneself with it.

From an Islamic perspective, the purpose of life is to "know and worship God."[30] Like Judaism and Christianity, Islam teaches that God made the world for a reason. To quote the Koran, "Our Lord! Thou hast not created this [the heavens and the earth] in vain!"[31] (Instead of "in vain," some scholars translate the end of this statement as "without purpose."[32])

From a Sikh standpoint, the purpose of life is to purify the mind and body so that we may become one with God. To quote the Granth Sahib, "The immortal status is obtained through [meditation on] the Name of the Lord; the mind and body become spotless and pure, which is the true purpose of life."[33]

Thus, although they differ in the details, many religious/philosophical traditions view life as profoundly purposeful. In this way, they align with the Jedi, who believe that "there is no such thing as luck."[34]

Chapter 14

SELFLESSNESS, RIGHT ACTION, AND KARMA

Various famous individuals have praised selflessness. For instance, the Fourteenth Dalai Lama (born in 1935) has said, "Our prime purpose in this life is to help others. And if you can't help them, at least don't hurt them."[1] Melissa de la Cruz (born in 1971), author of the *Blue Bloods* series, expresses a similar sentiment in her novel *Lost in Time*: "Maybe this was what love meant after all: sacrifice and selflessness . . . [and] the knowledge that another's well-being is more important than one's own."[2] Likewise, Veronica Roth (born in 1988), author of the best-selling *Divergent* trilogy, states the following in the first book of this trilogy: "There is power in self-sacrifice."[3]

These quotes correspond with principles in *Star Wars* and many religious/philosophical traditions.

SELFLESSNESS

Chapter 10 pointed out that the Jedi value selflessness. To quote Anakin Skywalker's words to Chancellor Palpatine in *Revenge of the Sith*, "The Jedi are selfless. . . . They only care about others."[4] As previously discussed, the Vedic tradition also praises this quality.

So do many other religious/philosophical traditions, such as Buddhism. The Dhammapada promotes generosity (also known as liberality), which is an aspect of selflessness. Here are a couple relevant quotes from this text: "A wise man rejoices in liberality"[5]; "Let a man . . . overcome the greedy by liberality"[6] (i.e., one should conquer miserliness with openhandedness).

Taoism also values selflessness. To quote the Tao Te Ching, "She [the Taoist master] gives no thought to self. / She is perfectly fulfilled."[7] In other words, Taoist masters are so deeply contented that they do not worry about their individual selves. Here is another pertinent quote from the same text: "The Master puts herself last; / And finds herself in the place of authority."[8] That is to say, Taoist masters place the needs of others before their own; as a result, people look to them as leaders.[9]

Likewise, various Native American and First Nations cultures encourage selflessness. For example, consider the following statements that promote generosity: "Sharing and giving are the ways of God" (Sauk proverb)[10]; "Life is both giving and receiving" (Mohawk proverb)[11]; "As children we are taught to give what we prize most, that we may taste the happiness of giving" (from Ohiyesa, aka Charles Alexander Eastman [1858–1939], a Santee Dakota writer).[12]

Judaism also praises selflessness. To quote the Book of Leviticus, "Do not seek revenge or bear a grudge against anyone among your people, but love your neighbor as yourself" (Lev. 19:18 NIV). In other words, we should care about others as much as we care about ourselves. Other biblical verses encourage generosity, such as the following: "The generous will themselves be blessed, for they share their food with the poor" (Prov. 22:9 NIV); "Give generously to them [your fellow Israelites] and do so without a grudging heart; then because of this the Lord your God will bless you in all your work and in everything you put your hand to" (Deut. 15:10 NIV).

The Christian New Testament contains many passages about the virtue of selflessness. For instance, in the Gospel of Luke, Jesus famously states, "Do to others as you would have them do to you" (Luke 6:31 NIV). In other words, we should treat others as we wish to be treated. Similarly, the Epistle to the Philippians urges Christians to "do nothing out of selfish ambition or vain conceit. Rather, in humility value others above yourselves, not looking to your own interests but each of you to the interests of the others" (Phil. 2:3–4 NIV). Thus, one should not selfishly put their own needs before the needs of others.

The Koran also discusses the merits of selflessness. For instance, it praises the people of Medina, an Islamic holy city, for their generous conduct toward immigrants:

> And those who made their abode in the city [the residents] and in the faith before them love those who have fled to them [the immigrants], and do not find in their hearts a need of what they are given, and prefer (them) before themselves though poverty may afflict them.[13]

According to this passage, the residents of Medina valued the needs of the immigrants above their own needs.

The Sikh Granth Sahib encourages selflessness as well: "Through selfless service, eternal peace is obtained."[14] Stated differently, if we serve others, this act will further our evolution toward higher states of consciousness.

Thus, many religious/philosophical traditions promote selflessness. The Jedi share the same ideal, considering selflessness an aspect of right action.

RIGHT ACTION

Chapter 7 also discussed the scene in *The Empire Strikes Back* in which Yoda warns the young Luke Skywalker about the dark side of the Force. In this scene, the Jedi Master explains to Luke how to discern between "the good side" and "the bad."[15]

We find similar themes in many religious/philosophical traditions, including Vedic teachings. Although these traditions sometimes disagree about what constitutes "good" and "bad," they agree on two points: (1) our actions matter, and (2) we should strive for righteousness and avoid wrongdoing. Consider the following examples.

The Buddhist Dhammapada emphasizes the importance of choosing right action over wrong action:

> Let no man think lightly of evil, saying in his heart, "It will not come nigh unto [near] me." Even by the falling of water-drops a water-pot is filled; the fool becomes full of evil, even if he gather it little by little.
>
> Let no man think lightly of good, saying in his heart, "It will not come nigh unto [near] me." Even by the falling of water-drops a water-pot is filled; the wise man becomes full of good, even if he gather it little by little.[16]

According to these verses, our actions—whether good or bad—have a cumulative effect; they gradually shape our character.

The Tao Te Ching associates right action with Taoist masters and other virtuous individuals: "Therefore the Master / does what she knows is right, / and makes no demands of others. / A virtuous person will do the right thing, / and persons with no virtue will take advantage of others."[17]

Various Native American and First Nations cultures urge us to act righteously. According to a proverb from the Zuni tribe, "The strong man walks with virtue."[18] We find a similar sentiment in a Hopi proverb, which states that we should "Be good to each other."[19]

The Hebrew Bible also values righteousness. To quote the Book of Psalms, "Even in darkness light dawns for the upright, for those who are gracious and compassionate and righteous" (Ps. 112:4 NIV). This verse suggests that even in difficult situations, there is still hope for the virtuous. Similarly, the Book of Proverbs discusses the benefits of righteousness: "Whoever pursues righteousness and love finds life, prosperity and honor" (Prov. 21:21 NIV). Simply stated, good attracts good—positive qualities lead to positive outcomes.

Likewise, the Christian New Testament urges the reader to "pursue righteousness," as well as "godliness, faith, love, endurance and gentleness" (1 Tim. 6:11 NIV). The First Epistle to the Thessalonians states, "Make sure that nobody pays back wrong for wrong, but always strive to do what is good for each other and for everyone else" (1 Thess. 5:15 NIV). In other words, we should never seek revenge; instead, we should always take the high road, as the saying goes.

Various Koranic statements also encourage righteousness, such as "Allah loves those who do good (to others)"[20] and "(As for) those who believe and do good, surely they are the best of men."[21] The practical takeaway is clear: We should always strive to live honorably.

The Sikh Granth Sahib contains similar themes, stating, "The one who commits sins lives in fear, while the one who lives righteously rejoices."[22] Thus, the penalty for wrongdoing is fear, and the reward for righteousness is joy. Another passage extols the pursuit of virtue: "The pursuit of virtue is my bow and arrow, my quiver, sword and scabbard. To be distinguished with honor is my drum and banner."[23]

In summary, although religious/philosophical traditions sometimes disagree about what constitutes right and wrong action, they agree that it is important to pursue virtue and avoid vice. In this way, they align with the Jedi, who seek to embody "the good" and shun "the bad."[24]

What happens when a person does the opposite, embodying "the bad" and shunning "the good"? Let's consider this topic next.

KARMA

Chapter 7 discussed how, in *Star Wars*, good eventually triumphs over evil. This theme is especially evident in the original trilogy and the sequel trilogy, in which the Jedi emerge victorious.

These events align with the Vedic principle of karma, which can be summarized as follows: "For every action, there is an equal and opposite reaction."[25] According to this principle, righteous, evolutionary action ultimately leads to positive results, whereas wrongful, non-evolutionary action leads to negative results.

Many religious/philosophical traditions contain similar concepts, as we will see in the following pages.

Like the Vedic tradition, Buddhism refers to karma. To quote the Dhammapada, "Fools of little understanding have themselves for their greatest enemies, for they do evil deeds which must bear bitter fruits."[26] In other words, those who engage in wrong actions ("evil deeds") experience undesirable outcomes ("bitter fruits"). These outcomes may not occur immediately: "An evil deed, like newly-drawn milk, does not turn (suddenly); smouldering, like fire covered by ashes, it follows the fool."[27] Thus, just as it takes time for milk to spoil, it can take a while for the results of past actions to play out. These actions are like "fire covered by ashes"—hidden, yet present.

Judaism and Christianity contain analogous concepts. To quote the Book of Job, "As I have observed, those who plow evil and those who sow trouble reap it" (Job 4:8 NIV). Similarly, the Epistle to the Galatians states, "A man reaps what he sows" (Gal. 6:7 NIV). If a farmer sows shriveled seeds, they will reap a poor harvest. Likewise, if we "sow" negative actions, we will "reap" negative results.

We find parallel themes in the Koran. For instance, this text states, "Whatever benefit comes to you (O man!), it is from Allah, and whatever misfortune befalls you, it is from yourself."[28] This verse implies that misfortune is the consequence of our actions. Now, there may also be other factors at play. To quote Islamic scholar Mustafa Khattab, "In some cases, bad things happen to good people to test their faith . . . or as part of a process of replacing something with what is better (e.g., a job or a spouse)."[29]

Like the religious/philosophical traditions already mentioned, Sikhism teaches that actions have consequences. To quote the Granth Sahib, "The body is the field of karma in this age; whatever you plant, you shall harvest."[30] This statement seems to be a variation of the biblical principle that "a man reaps what he sows" (Gal. 6:7 NIV). From a Sikh perspective, we can escape negative karma through meditation, which can remove "the filth of lifetimes of karma."[31]

Thus, many religious/philosophical traditions refer to karma or a related concept. In this way, they correspond with *Star Wars*, which indicates that good will eventually triumph over evil.

Chapter 15

INTUITION, NON-ATTACHMENT, AND POSITIVITY

Various famous individuals have discussed the value of intuition. For instance, Albert Einstein (1879–1955) remarked, "I believe in intuitions and inspirations. . . . I sometimes *feel* that I am right. I do not *know* that I am."[1] *New York Times* best-selling novelist Dean Koontz (born in 1945) has also commented on this mental faculty: "Intuition is seeing with the soul."[2] Likewise, influential author C. JoyBell C. refers to intuition as one of the "senses of our souls."[3]

In *Star Wars*, the Jedi value intuition. So do many religious/philosophical traditions, as we will see in the following section.

INTUITION

Chapter 8 noted that intuition is an important theme in *Star Wars*, as illustrated by the following quotes: "I have a very bad feeling about this"[4] and "Search your feelings."[5] We find the same theme in the Vedic tradition, which teaches that "through intuition everything can be known."[6]

Many other religious/philosophical traditions also discuss intuition or a related concept, as we will see in this section.

Scholar Akihisa Kondo comments on the significance of intuition in Zen Buddhism:

> According to our Oriental concept it is understood that intuition is one of the deepest functions of the human mind. It is a means of perceiving reality directly, not by means of logic or reasoning. This occurs or is experienced when the personality is well-integrated.[7]

Taoism also contains the principle of intuition. The Taoist priest Ted Kardash urges us to value this mental faculty. He explains that "insight, discovery, and creativity all come from a place beyond the logical mind."[8] The Tao Te Ching seems to refer to this "place" in the following quote: "Use your inner light for understanding,"[9] suggesting that we can access the truth by looking within.

Various Native American and First Nations cultures discuss similar concepts. To quote a Lakota prayer:

> Wakan Tanka, Great Mystery, teach me how to trust my heart, my mind, my intuition, my inner knowing, the senses of my body, the blessings of my spirit. Teach me to trust these things so that I may enter my Sacred Space and love beyond my fear, and thus Walk in Balance with the passing of each glorious Sun.[10]

This prayer implies that a balanced life depends on trusting our essential human faculties, including "intuition" and "inner knowing."

Unlike most of the sources mentioned thus far, the Hebrew Bible does not refer to intuition by name; however, it contains a related concept: insight. "Insight" means "the capacity to gain an accurate and deep intuitive understanding of a person or thing."[11] Here are two biblical verses on this topic: (1) "God gave Solomon wisdom and very great insight, and a breadth of understanding as measureless as the sand on the seashore" (1 Kings 4:29 NIV); (2) "How much better to get wisdom than gold, to get insight rather than silver!" (Prov. 16:16 NIV).

The Christian New Testament includes parallel verses. For instance, the Epistle to the Philippians states, "And this is my prayer: that your love may abound more and more in knowledge and depth of insight" (Phil. 1:9 NIV). Such insight has practical benefits; it allows one to "discern what is best" in life (Phil. 1:10 NIV). The Second Epistle to Timothy comments on the same topic: "Reflect on what I am saying, for the Lord will give you insight into all this" (2 Tim. 2:7 NIV). This verse suggests that divinely inspired insight can shed light on religious teachings.

In Islam, the Sufis (mystics) place importance on *kashf*, which is analogous to intuition. *Kashf* may be defined as "the privileged inner knowledge that mystics acquire through personal experience and direct vision of God."[12] To emphasize, this knowledge is gained through direct experience, not intellectual reasoning. The prominent Muslim theologian Al-Ghazali (died in 1111) describes *kashf* as "a light with which God floods the heart of the believer."[13]

In Sikhism, the Granth Sahib discusses intuition: "The Lord entrusts the treasures of peace, intuition and kindness to His devotees."[14] Likewise, another passage calls God "the Giver of peace and intuition."[15] One may receive these divine gifts through meditation.

Thus, many religious/philosophical traditions refer to intuition or a related concept. These teachings recall the Jedi, who often rely on intuition.

(To reiterate, this mental faculty is not to be confused with everyday emotions. Emotions may lead us astray, whereas intuition provides a solid basis for action.)

NON-ATTACHMENT

Chapter 8 also discussed the theme of non-attachment in *Star Wars*, bringing up *Revenge of the Sith*, in which Yoda warns Anakin Skywalker about the harmful effects of attachment. Unfortunately, Anakin fails to heed this warning, which contributes to his fall to the dark side of the Force.

Similar to *Star Wars*, the Vedic tradition portrays attachment as one of the main causes of suffering. It encourages us to avoid this tendency by meditating and thereby experiencing the state of eternal bliss consciousness (*sat chit ananda*). Through regular practice, this state can become permanent; at this point, the individual is so filled with bliss that they are not attached to anything.

Other religious/philosophical traditions, such as Buddhism, also contain the principle of non-attachment. For instance, consider the three following quotes from the Dhammapada.

> Dhammapada 89: "Those whose mind is well grounded . . . who without clinging to anything, rejoice in freedom from attachment, whose appetites have been conquered, and who are full of light, are free (even) in this world."[16] According to this verse, it is possible to live in this world while remaining unattached to it.
>
> Dhammapada 401: "Him I call indeed a Brahmana [a holy person] who does not cling to pleasures, like water on a lotus leaf, like a mustard seed on the point of a needle."[17] Thus, a holy person is not attached to superficial pleasures, just as a drop of water is not attached to a lotus leaf (it can easily roll off).
>
> Dhammapada 414: "Him I call indeed a Brahmana who has traversed this miry road, the impassable world and its vanity, who has gone through, and reached the other shore, is thoughtful, guileless, free

from doubts, free from attachment, and content."[18] According to this verse, holy people have transcended attachment to this world and found contentment within. Buddhism recommends that we meditate to attain this goal.

Sikhism includes the principle of non-attachment as well. To quote the Granth Sahib, "Whatever is seen shall pass away. So do not be attached to this false show. Like a traveller [*sic*] in his travels, you have come. Behold the caravan leaving each day."[19] In other words, we should not cling to this world because it is not our permanent home. Instead, we should meditate and thereby develop a natural state of non-attachment.

Now, there are different kinds of attachment, including attachment to material possessions. Many religious/philosophical traditions warn against this tendency. They suggest that it is all right to have possessions but caution us not to place undue importance on them.

For example, take Taoism. According to the Tao Te Ching, the Taoist master "has without possessing"; in other words, they have belongings but are not attached to them. Furthermore, the Taoist master avoids "the crime of excess," which is "to waste all of your money buying possessions." These quotes indicate that there are worthwhile uses for one's money other than acquiring material items. The Tao Te Ching reminds us to keep our priorities straight by asking, "Which is more valuable, your possessions or your person?" It warns that there is "no greater retribution than for greed."[20] In other words, greed (the "intense and selfish desire for something"[21]) leads to negative consequences.

Similarly, the Hebrew Bible and the Christian New Testament caution against excessive attachment to worldly belongings. The Hebrew Bible states, "Those who trust in their riches will fall, but the righteous will thrive like a green leaf" (Prov. 11:28 NIV). Likewise, the New Testament urges us to "keep your lives free from the love of money and be content with what you have, because God has said, 'Never will I leave you; never will I forsake you'" (Heb. 13:5 NIV). These verses do not necessarily indicate that money and riches are bad; however, they do imply that there are more important things in life.

The Koran conveys a similar message, reminding us that wealth won't bring us immortality: "Woe to every slanderer, defamer, who amasses wealth and considers it a provision (against mishap); he thinks that his wealth will make him immortal."[22]

The Sikh Granth Sahib likewise emphasizes the limitations of wealth: "Riches do not remain with anyone"[23] (i.e., we can't take them with us when we die). Therefore, we shouldn't spend all our time in the pursuit of wealth; we should also engage in spiritual practices like meditation. These practices lead to a different kind of wealth: "Those who gather Truth, and the riches of the Lord's Name, are rich and very fortunate."[24]

Likewise, the Vedic tradition warns against attachment to worldly riches. To quote the Katha Upanishad, "Unaware of his own mortality, the childish one / stumbles about, enchanted by the folly of riches."[25] This verse suggests that people may be so engrossed by material possessions that they lose sight of more important things. Fortunately, meditation can help them gain a clearer sense of priorities.

Like the religious/philosophical traditions already mentioned, Buddhism looks down on greed (meaning the "intense and selfish desire for something, especially wealth, power, or food"[26]). Here are some verses on this topic from the Dhammapada:

"Let us live happily then, free from greed among the greedy! Among men who are greedy let us dwell free from greed!"

"From greed comes grief, from greed comes fear; he who is free from greed knows neither grief nor fear."

"O man, know this, that the unrestrained [i.e., those who lack restraint] are in a bad state; take care that greediness and vice do not bring thee to grief for a long time!"[27]

Certain Native American and First Nations figures seem not to have been motivated by greed; they considered material possessions relatively unimportant. Take the following quote by Red Cloud (1822–1909), an Oglala Lakota leader: "We do not want riches, we want peace and love."[28]

In summary, some religious/philosophical traditions, such as the Vedic tradition, Buddhism, and Sikhism, contain the principle of non-attachment. Furthermore, many traditions caution against attachment to material possessions, encouraging us to remember what's important in life. The Jedi hold similar views on these topics, as evidenced by their modest lifestyles and Yoda's warnings to Anakin in *Revenge of the Sith*.

We might say that the opposite of attachment is letting go, which is also a key theme in *Star Wars*. To use the Force, Luke Skywalker must "let go" of his conscious self.[29] Likewise, to return to the light side, Darth Vader must "let go" of his hate.[30]

As discussed earlier, the Vedic tradition contains parallel concepts. According to this tradition, we need to let go of attachment, individual limitations, and the ignorance of our true nature. We can achieve these goals by enlivening the state of eternal bliss consciousness through meditation.

Many other religious/philosophical traditions urge us to let go of negative tendencies, as we will see in the following paragraphs.

In Buddhism, the Dhammapada encourages us to overcome anger and other harmful traits: "Let a man overcome anger by love, let him overcome evil by good; let him overcome the greedy by liberality, the liar by truth!"[31] Thus, to conquer anger, evil, greed, and untruth, we should cultivate the opposites of these qualities, which is possible through meditation.

In Taoism, the Tao Te Ching implies that we should let go of the impulse to control the world:

> Do you want to rule the world and control it?
> I don't think it can ever be done.
> The world is a sacred vessel
> and it can not [*sic*] be controlled.
> You will only make it worse if you try.
> It may slip through your fingers and disappear.[32]

From a Taoist perspective, instead of attempting to rule the world, we should seek to act in harmony with it.

The scriptures of Judaism and Christianity urge us to overcome selfishness. The Hebrew Bible contains the following prayer: "Turn my heart toward your [God's] statutes and not toward selfish gain" (Ps. 119:36 NIV). Likewise, the New Testament states, "Do nothing out of selfish ambition or vain conceit. Rather, in humility value others above yourselves" (Phil. 2:3 NIV).

In Islam, the Koran expresses similar themes. It praises the generous conduct of the people of Medina, concluding that those who overcome selfishness "are the successful ones."[33] In other words, true success depends on conquering egocentric tendencies.

We find analogous statements in the Sikh Granth Sahib, which encourages us to "eradicate selfishness and conceit from within."[34] One may reach this goal through meditation, which allows "the Divine Light" to dispel the darkness within them.[35]

In summary, many religious/philosophical traditions urge us to let go of negative tendencies. These teachings are reminiscent of the Jedi, who strive to overcome harmful traits like anger, fear, and aggression.

It is easier to achieve these goals if we believe it is possible to do so; a positive mindset can be a powerful tool. Let's turn to this topic next.

POSITIVITY

Chapter 10 discussed the scene in *The Empire Strikes Back* in which Yoda Force-lifts Luke Skywalker's starship from the swamp. Why does Yoda succeed at this task while Luke fails? Because the young man believes it is impossible, whereas the Jedi Master knows that all things are possible through the Force. In other words, Luke's negative mindset leads to negative results, whereas Yoda's positive mindset leads to positive results. This scene depicts the power of positivity.

We find similar themes in many religious/philosophical traditions (including the Vedic tradition). Let's consider some examples.

Various Native American and First Nations cultures urge us to focus on the positive. To quote a Cree proverb, "Be truthful and respectful in our speech, which in itself is a miracle and a gift from the Creator, that we might use it only to speak good of each other and pass on the good things of life."[36] According to this proverb, we should use our words to enliven "the good things" in life.

Similarly, the Hebrew Bible encourages us to think and speak positively. For example, take the following verses: "A cheerful heart is good medicine, but a crushed spirit dries up the bones" (Prov. 17:22 NIV); "Gracious words are a honeycomb, sweet to the soul and healing to the bones" (Prov. 16:24 NIV); "Anxiety weighs down the heart, but a kind word cheers it up" (Prov. 12:25 NIV).

Likewise, the Christian New Testament advises us to be attentive to the best things in life. To quote the Epistle to the Philippians, "Finally, brothers and sisters, whatever is true, whatever is noble, whatever is right, whatever is pure, whatever is lovely, whatever is admirable—if anything is excellent or praiseworthy—think about such things" (Phil. 4:8 NIV).

The Koran places importance on gratitude, which involves focusing on the positive. According to this text, "Allah will reward the grateful."[37] Similarly, a subsequent chapter states, "[The Lord proclaimed:] 'If you are grateful, I would certainly give to you more.'"[38] These verses suggest that if we count our blessings, they will multiply.

The Sikh Granth Sahib also encourages gratitude and positivity: "Forever and ever, night and day, I praise the Greatness of Your [the Lord's] Goodness. You bestow Your Gifts, even if we do not ask for them."[39] This passage emphasizes the divine gifts we receive as opposed to the challenges we face.

The Buddhist Dhammapada and the Taoist Tao Te Ching do not discuss positivity in the same way as the texts mentioned earlier; nonetheless, they contain many uplifting themes. For instance, they teach that it is possible to cultivate a lasting state of contentment. The Dhammapada refers to holy people as "thoughtful, guileless, free from doubts, free from attachment, and *content.*"[40] Likewise, the Tao Te Ching remarks, "Whoever knows contentment will be at peace forever."[41] How to achieve this state of inner fulfillment? Through meditation, which is found in both the Buddhist and the Taoist traditions.

To recap, many religious/philosophical traditions value positivity. In this regard, they are like Yoda, who teaches Luke to view the world with greater optimism.

Chapter 16

KNOWLEDGE AND STRENGTH OF MIND

Which is more powerful: a strong body or a strong mind? Clearly the latter—from a Jedi perspective. Yoda is the perfect example of this principle. Physically, he is small, old, and frail; mentally, however, he is so strong with the Force that he can perform incredible feats like lifting Luke's starship out of the swamp in *The Empire Strikes Back*.

Like the Jedi, many religious/philosophical traditions, including the Vedic tradition, value strength of mind.

STRENGTH OF MIND

In Buddhism, strength of mind is associated with wisdom. The Dhammapada compares "wise people" to "a solid rock" that "is not shaken by the wind"[1]—an analogy that denotes strength: "As a solid rock is not shaken by the wind, wise people falter not amidst blame and praise. / Wise people, after they have listened to the laws [the teachings of the Buddha], become serene, like a deep, smooth, and still lake."[2]

According to Taoism, strength of mind comes from self-mastery, which can be attained through meditation. To quote the Tao Te Ching, "Those who master others are strong; / those who master themselves have true power."[3]

Various Native American and First Nations cultures also value strength of mind. Ohiyesa (aka Charles Alexander Eastman), a Santee Dakota writer, comments on this topic: "The man who preserves his selfhood ever calm and unshaken by the storms of existence . . . [has] the ideal attitude and conduct of life."[4] Likewise, a Cherokee prayer refers to inner peace, which

119

seems to be an aspect of strong-mindedness: "O' Great Spirit, help me always . . . to remember the peace that may be found in silence."[5]

From a Jewish perspective, strength of mind comes from God. For illustration, consider the following verses from the Hebrew Bible: "My flesh and my heart may fail, but God is the strength of my heart and my portion forever" (Ps. 73:26 NIV); "He [God] gives strength to the weary and increases the power of the weak" (Isa. 40:29 NIV); "So do not fear, for I am with you; do not be dismayed, for I am your God. I will strengthen you and help you; I will uphold you with my righteous right hand" (Isa. 41:10 NIV).

The Christian New Testament contains parallel verses. To quote the Epistle to the Ephesians, "I pray that out of his glorious riches he [God] may strengthen you with power through his Spirit in your inner being" (Eph. 3:16 NIV). Similarly, the Epistle to the Philippians states, "I can do all this through him [Jesus Christ] who gives me strength" (Phil. 4:13 NIV).

In a similar vein, the Koran implies that the Lord can increase our strength: "He [God] will send on you clouds pouring down abundance of rain and add strength to your strength."[6]

We find the same concepts in the Sikh Granth Sahib, which contains the following statements: "The Lord infuses strength"[7] and "[O Lord,] I stand tall; You are my Strength."[8] This strength can be gained from within, for God is "inside of all."[9]

Thus, like the Jedi, many religious/philosophical traditions value strength of mind.

Now, the stronger one's mind, the more capable one will be of discerning between true knowledge and falsehood, which leads to our next topic: knowledge.

KNOWLEDGE

Chapter 9 pointed out that the Jedi hold the following views regarding knowledge: (1) it is immensely valuable; (2) it can be gained from within; (3) it should be supplemented by experience; and (4) the opposite of knowledge—namely, ignorance—must be overcome.

Many religious/philosophical traditions, including the Vedic tradition, contain the same principles. Let's consider some examples.

Buddhism includes all the concepts listed previously. In this tradition, knowledge is associated with "the four truths of the noble ones," which may be summarized as follows: "Suffering exists; it has a cause; it has an end; and it has a cause to bring about its end."[10] Suffering can be overcome by following "the eightfold path of the noble ones," which consists of "right view, right resolve, right speech, right conduct, right livelihood, right effort, right mindfulness, and right 'samadhi' (meditative absorption or union)."[11]

Like Buddhism, Taoism emphasizes the importance of inner knowledge. To quote the Tao Te Ching, "How do I know where creation comes from? / I look inside myself and see it."[12] In other words, we can discover the source of creation—the Tao—by looking within through meditation.

Similarly, various Native American and First Nations cultures teach that knowledge can be gained from within. To return to the Lakota prayer mentioned in the previous chapter:

> Wakan Tanka, Great Mystery, teach me how to trust my heart, my mind, my intuition, *my inner knowing*, the senses of my body, the blessings of my spirit. Teach me to trust these things so that I may enter my Sacred Space and love beyond my fear, and thus Walk in Balance with the passing of each glorious Sun.[13]

This prayer suggests that human beings possess an innate sense of knowing.

Like the traditions already mentioned, Judaism and Christianity value knowledge. For example, consider these biblical verses: "The wise store up knowledge, but the mouth of a fool invites ruin" (Prov. 10:14 NIV); "The heart of the discerning acquires knowledge, for the ears of the wise seek it out" (Prov. 18:15 NIV); "For wisdom will enter your heart, and knowledge will be pleasant to your soul" (Prov. 2:10 NIV); "For the Lord gives wisdom; from his mouth come knowledge and understanding" (Prov. 2:6 NIV).

The Koran also alludes to the value of knowledge, as we see in the following excerpt: "He [God] it is Who made the sun a shining brightness and the moon a light, and ordained for it mansions [phases] *that you might know* the computation of years and the reckoning."[14] This verse suggests that God created the universe in an orderly fashion so people could understand how it functions.

Like many of the religious/philosophical traditions already discussed, Sikhism teaches that knowledge can be gained from within. To quote the Granth Sahib, "Deep within, the Divine Light has dawned, and the darkness of ignorance has been dispelled."[15] This quote seems to describe a profound spiritual experience.

In summary, like the Jedi, many religious/philosophical traditions hold the following views regarding knowledge: (1) it is immensely valuable; (2) it can be gained from within; (3) it should be supplemented by experience; and (4) the opposite of knowledge—namely, ignorance—must be overcome.

Chapter 17

SPIRITUALITY AND REDEMPTION

As human beings, we often identify ourselves by our age, gender, cultural background, occupation, relationship status, and so forth. Yet, according to many religious/philosophical traditions, we are more than any of these things; our true essence transcends our physical form and our social position. Let's explore this topic and its *Star Wars* parallels.

SPIRITUAL BEINGS

Chapter 10 discussed Yoda's remark, "Luminous beings are we . . . not this crude matter."[1] This quote implies that we are more than our bodies. It corresponds with the following statement, which is of uncertain origin: "You are not a human being having a spiritual experience. You are a spiritual being having a human experience."[2]

Many religious/philosophical traditions, including the Vedic tradition, agree that we are more than our bodies. Let's consider some examples.

According to Taoism, we are not just localized physical entities; rather, we are "one of the countless manifestations of the Tao."[3] In other words, we are part of the "universal essence."[4] Therefore, we will never truly perish; to quote scholar Bernard Down, "Man may die indeed, but his essence as part of the universal essence lives on forever."[5]

Similar to Taoism, Judaism and Christianity teach that we are not merely physical but also spiritual in nature. These Western religions assert that we were created in the image and likeness of God, who is a spiritual being. Here are two quotes on this topic from the Hebrew Bible: "God

created mankind in his own image" (Gen. 1:27 NIV) and "When God created mankind, he made them in the likeness of God" (Gen. 5:1 NIV).

The Christian New Testament discusses the spiritual aspect of human
nature as well. For instance, take the following verse from the First Epistle
to the Corinthians: "Do you not know that you are the temple of God and
that the Spirit of God dwells in you?" (1 Cor. 3:16 NKJV).

Likewise, the Islamic Sufis (mystics) indicate that we are spiritual
beings. To quote the Sufi poet Rumi, "Although you appear in earthly form
/ Your essence is pure Consciousness."[6]

Similarly, Sikhism teaches that we are essentially the same as God, who
is a spiritual being. To quote the Granth Sahib, "There is only one breath; all
are made of the same clay; the light within all is the same. The One Light
pervades all the many and various beings."[7] In other words, the light of God
is within all beings.

Thus, many religious/philosophical traditions assert that we are
not merely physical in nature. As previously discussed, the Jedi share the
same view.

Although we may be spiritual beings, we do not always act in an
evolutionary manner. Fortunately, when we err, we have the possibility of
gaining redemption—that is, according to *Star Wars* and various religious/
philosophical traditions.

REDEMPTION

Chapter 10 also discussed the theme of redemption in *Star Wars*, which is
personified by Anakin Skywalker (aka Darth Vader) and Ben Solo (aka Kylo
Ren). Both characters fall into darkness and then rise again into the light.

Like *Star Wars*, many religious/philosophical traditions, including the
Vedic tradition, refer to redemption or a related principle. Let's look at
some examples.

The Buddhist version of redemption is the attainment of *nirvana*
(enlightenment), a state beyond sin. To quote the Dhammapada, "He who
has tasted the sweetness of solitude and tranquillity [*sic*; qualities of *nirvana*],
is free from fear and free from sin."[8] In theory, one may achieve this goal
through regular meditation.

Taoism refers to redemption in the Ten Precepts, a list of rules for
practitioners. The second precept states, "Broadly reach out to bring universal redemption to all!"[9] This quote implies that redemption is within
everyone's reach.

From a Jewish perspective, redemption comes from God, as evidenced by the following verse from the Hebrew Bible: "Israel, put your hope in the Lord, for with the Lord is unfailing love and with him is full redemption. He himself will redeem Israel from all their sins" (Ps. 130:7–8 NIV).

Christianity emphasizes the role of Jesus Christ in bringing redemption. To quote the New Testament, "In him [Christ] we have redemption through his blood, the forgiveness of sins, in accordance with the riches of God's grace" (Eph. 1:7 NIV). According to most Christians, Christ atoned for the sins of humankind through his death and resurrection.

Islam also contains the principle of redemption, as illustrated by the following verse from the Koran: "And (as to) those who do evil deeds, then repent after that and believe, your Lord after that is most surely Forgiving, Merciful."[10] In other words, one may gain redemption through repentance and correct belief.

Redemption is an important tenet in Sikhism as well. The Granth Sahib refers to God as the "Redeemer of sinners," stating that "all sins and misdeeds shall be erased" through meditation on the name of the Lord.[11]

In summary, many religious/philosophical traditions refer to redemption or a related principle. In this way, they align with *Star Wars*, which depicts the redemption of both Anakin Skywalker and Ben Solo.

Chapter 18

THE BIG PICTURE

In this final chapter, let's return to the question asked at the beginning of the book: Why do people love *Star Wars*? Of course, they appreciate the characters, the plot, the music, and the special effects.

However, there may be a deeper reason why these films resonate with audiences: Perhaps *Star Wars* contains universal truths (i.e., principles that are "true for all time, all places and all people"[1]). Furthermore, perhaps the same principles can be found in many religious/philosophical traditions, as evidenced by the parallels discussed in the previous chapters.

The next section lists these proposed universal truths. It includes two versions of each principle: one in *Star Wars* terminology and one in religious/philosophical terminology. (In some cases, the two versions are identical.)

EIGHTEEN UNIVERSAL TRUTHS

1. *Star Wars*: There is an all-pervading Force.
   Various religious/philosophical traditions: There is an all-pervading level of reality that may be called "*Brahman*," "the Tao," "God," or "the Great Spirit."

2. *Star Wars*: The Force is within the Jedi.
   Various religious/philosophical traditions: *Brahman*/the Tao/the kingdom of God/the Great Spirit is within human beings.

3. *Star Wars*: One may connect with the Force through meditation.

Various religious/philosophical traditions: One may connect with *Brahman*/the Tao/God/the Great Spirit through meditation and/or prayer.

4. *Star Wars*: One may gain support from the Force.
Various religious/philosophical traditions: One may gain support from *Brahman*/God/the Great Spirit.

5. *Star Wars*: Life is an interplay between the light and dark sides of the Force.
Various religious/philosophical traditions: Life is an interplay between opposites (light and darkness, *yin* and *yang*, etc.).

6. *Star Wars*: It is important to maintain the balance between the light and dark sides of the Force.
Various religious/philosophical traditions: It is important to maintain balance in life.

7. *Star Wars*: Anger, fear, and aggression lead to the dark side of the Force.
Various religious/philosophical traditions: Anger, fear, and aggression are negative tendencies that should be overcome.

8. *Star Wars*: Death is inevitable, but immortality is attainable.
Various religious/philosophical traditions: Death is inevitable, but immortality is attainable.

9. *Star Wars*: "There is no such thing as luck."[2]
Various religious/philosophical traditions: Life is purposeful, not random or accidental.

10. *Star Wars*: We should aim to act righteously and selflessly.
Various religious/philosophical traditions: We should aim to act righteously and selflessly.

11. *Star Wars*: Good will eventually triumph over evil.
Various religious/philosophical traditions: Good actions will bring positive karma, and evil actions will bring negative karma—"A man reaps what he sows" (Gal. 6:7 NIV).

12. *Star Wars*: Intuition is a valuable tool.
Various religious/philosophical traditions: Intuition is a valuable tool.

13. *Star Wars*: Attachment can lead to suffering.
Various religious/philosophical traditions: Attachment can lead to suffering.

14. *Star Wars*: Positivity is a desirable trait.
Various religious/philosophical traditions: Positivity is a desirable trait.

15. *Star Wars*: Strength of mind is also desirable.
Various religious/philosophical traditions: Strength of mind is also desirable.

16. *Star Wars*: It is important to seek knowledge and overcome ignorance.
Various religious/philosophical traditions: It is important to seek knowledge and overcome ignorance.

17. *Star Wars*: "Luminous beings are we . . . not this crude matter."[3]
Various religious/philosophical traditions: We are spiritual beings.

18. *Star Wars*: If we have erred, it is possible to find redemption.
Various religious/philosophical traditions: If we have erred, it is possible to find redemption.

Again, based on the previous chapters, I propose that these eighteen concepts are universal truths—regardless of whether we express them in *Star Wars* terminology or religious/philosophical terminology.

Let's consider some practical takeaways from this proposal.

PRACTICAL TAKEAWAYS

1. *Star Wars*: **There is an all-pervading Force.**

Various religious/philosophical traditions: There is an all-pervading level of reality that may be called "Brahman," "the Tao," "God," or "the Great Spirit."

If this principle were true, then the omnipresent level of reality would connect all beings and objects, just as the broth connects all the ingredients in a soup. As part of this "soup," each person would be linked to everyone and everything else—from the squirrel in their backyard to their neighbor down the street to a stranger in a foreign country.

Due to this interconnectedness, one's actions would have far-reaching effects. Every choice would be like tossing a stone into a pond; the ripples would spread across the entire surface. If one treated people kindly and fairly, this act would create "ripples" of harmony in the world around them; if they dealt with others harshly and unjustly, it would produce the opposite result.

Here is a practical takeaway from these concepts: We should be mindful of our actions. From time to time, we should ask ourselves, "Are these the kinds of 'ripples' I want to create in the world?" If the answer is no, then we should modify our behavior.

Here is another takeaway: If the Force/*Brahman*/the Tao/God/the Great Spirit is everywhere, then we don't need to go anywhere to find it. We can feel its presence at home or in nature, not just in traditional places of worship. There is nothing wrong with attending a church, a synagogue, a mosque, or a temple; however, the Force/*Brahman*/the Tao/God/the Great Spirit is not restricted to these locations.

2. *Star Wars*: The Force is within the Jedi.

Various religious/philosophical traditions: Brahman/the Tao/the kingdom of God/ the Great Spirit is within human beings.

This principle reinforces the idea that we don't have to go anywhere to find the Force/*Brahman*/the Tao/the kingdom of God/the Great Spirit— because it is already within us! All we need is a means of revealing its presence, such as meditation or prayer.

This principle also implies that the same Force/*Brahman*/Tao/kingdom of God/Great Spirit exists within all human beings. This idea creates a sense of unity with others. It encourages us to focus on our profound similarities versus our superficial differences.

3. *Star Wars*: One may connect with the Force through meditation.

Various religious/philosophical traditions: One may connect with Brahman/the Tao/ God/the Great Spirit through meditation and/or prayer.

This principle suggests that we don't have to blindly believe in the Force/*Brahman*/the Tao/God/the Great Spirit; instead, we can experience this level of reality firsthand through meditation and/or prayer. (For information about different styles of meditation, please go to appendix A.)

4. *Star Wars*: One may gain support from the Force.

Various religious/philosophical traditions: One may gain support from Brahman/God/the Great Spirit.

In other words, by connecting with the Force/*Brahman*/God/the Great Spirit through meditation and/or prayer, we may achieve greater success in life.

5. *Star Wars*: Life is an interplay between the light and dark sides of the Force.

Various religious/philosophical traditions: Life is an interplay between opposites (light and darkness, yin and yang, etc.).

Here is a takeaway from this principle: As human beings, we can support one opposite over another. For instance, we can promote righteousness and discourage wrongdoing, thereby improving our world.

6. *Star Wars*: It is important to maintain the balance between the light and dark sides of the Force.

Various religious/philosophical traditions: It is important to maintain balance in life.

We can apply this principle on physical, mental, and spiritual levels. On a physical level, we should strive for balance in our diet and daily routine. On a mental level, we should seek balance between work and play, alone time and social activities, and so forth. On a spiritual level, we can attain an inner state of balance through meditation, which can prepare us for whatever life brings our way.

7. *Star Wars*: Anger, fear, and aggression lead to the dark side of the Force.

Various religious/philosophical traditions: Anger, fear, and aggression are negative tendencies that should be overcome.

How to conquer these tendencies? From a Vedic perspective, we should meditate and experience the state of eternal bliss consciousness, which will naturally reduce anger, fear, and aggression. (Other religious/philosophical traditions may recommend different approaches.)

8. *Star Wars*: Death is inevitable, but immortality is attainable.

Various religious/philosophical traditions: Death is inevitable, but immortality is attainable.

The inevitability of death should encourage us to make the most of life. As Steve Jobs noted in his 2005 commencement address at Stanford University, our "time is limited"[4]; therefore, we shouldn't waste it. Instead, we should decide what is important to us and channel our energy toward that.

If immortality is possible, then we should seek knowledge of how to attain it from a religious/philosophical tradition that resonates with us. According to the Vedic tradition, the key is to meditate and gain union with eternal bliss consciousness, which is everlasting.

9. *Star Wars*: "There is no such thing as luck."[5]

Various religious/philosophical traditions: Life is purposeful, not random or accidental.

If this idea is true, then we should try to discover the purpose of life. Different religious/philosophical traditions hold different views on this topic, so we should search for an explanation that makes sense to us. Then we should align our actions with that purpose.

For example, suppose that we accept the following Vedic teaching: the goal of life is to attain higher states of consciousness. We can align our actions with this goal by meditating, maintaining a healthy lifestyle, following our personal *dharma*, treating others well, and otherwise behaving in the most evolutionary manner possible.

10. *Star Wars*: We should aim to act righteously and selflessly.

Various religious/philosophical traditions: We should aim to act righteously and selflessly.

Here, the simplest takeaway is to follow the Golden Rule: "Do to others as you would have them do to you" (Luke 6:31 NIV). In other words, we should treat others as we would want to be treated. George Lucas endorses this rule, calling it "the philosophy that permeates my work."[6]

There are countless ways to apply the Golden Rule. We can strive to be agreeable even when we are tired. We can listen carefully to our friends and family, even when they are discussing topics we don't find compelling. We can admit fault when we have fallen short in some way. And so on.

11. *Star Wars*: Good will eventually triumph over evil.

Various religious/philosophical traditions: Good actions will bring positive karma, and evil actions will bring negative karma—"A man reaps what he sows" (Gal. 6:7 NIV).

This principle may inspire us to take a stand against wrongdoing. It suggests that virtue is sustainable and vice unsustainable, since no one can outrun karma forever. This idea would mean that the injustices in our world are only temporary, which is a comforting thought.

12. *Star Wars*: Intuition is a valuable tool.

Various religious/philosophical traditions: Intuition is a valuable tool.

Sometimes we may hear a quiet voice inside guiding us toward (or away from) a particular path. This "path" could symbolize a job, a relationship, a geographical location, and so forth. The inner voice may be our intuition, so it is worth considering what it has to say.

We should be careful when applying this principle, however, as intuition can be confused with everyday emotions, which are often unreliable. Therefore, it is best to analyze our impulses in light of common sense before acting on them.

13. *Star Wars*: Attachment can lead to suffering.

Various religious/philosophical traditions: Attachment can lead to suffering.

How can we avoid attachment? From a Vedic perspective, the key is to meditate and experience the state of eternal bliss consciousness. Through regular practice, we can become so filled with bliss that we are not attached to anything. (Other religious/philosophical traditions may prescribe different approaches.)

14. *Star Wars*: **Positivity is a desirable trait.**

Various religious/philosophical traditions: Positivity is a desirable trait.

The simplest takeaway from this principle is to focus on the positive. This task shouldn't be too difficult, as most of us have a lot to be grateful for—we have a roof over our heads, food on the table, and family/friends who care about us. It is helpful to remember these facts whenever negative thoughts dominate our awareness.

Here is another takeaway: We may want to consider ways to naturally increase our positivity, such as through meditation.

15. *Star Wars*: **Strength of mind is also desirable.**

Various religious/philosophical traditions: Strength of mind is also desirable.

This principle again brings to light the value of meditation, which can naturally increase our strength of mind.

16. *Star Wars*: **It is important to seek knowledge and overcome ignorance.**

Various religious/philosophical traditions: It is important to seek knowledge and overcome ignorance.

Knowledge is empowering. This statement applies to both practical and theoretical knowledge. Let's consider an example of each. On a practical level, if we understand how to manage our finances, we will be more capable of weathering economic turmoil. On a theoretical level, if we comprehend the purpose of existence, we will have a clearer sense of how to live meaningful lives.

17. *Star Wars*: **"Luminous beings are we . . . not this crude matter."**[7]

Various religious/philosophical traditions: We are spiritual beings.

As noted previously, this principle means that we are more than our bodies. Indeed, there are different layers to our existence: physical, mental, and spiritual. Of these layers, the physical is the most superficial.

If this idea is true, then we should place less importance on how we look and more on how we think and act. What really matters is not our appearance but how we choose to engage with the world.

18. *Star Wars*: **If we have erred, it is possible to find redemption.**

Various religious/philosophical traditions: If we have erred, it is possible to find redemption.

We have all made mistakes, but based on this principle, we aren't permanently tainted by our past; we can transcend our former limitations and become better human beings. Most religious/philosophical traditions agree on these points, though they prescribe different ways to attain redemption.

★★★

To recap, the previous section listed eighteen concepts that are found in both *Star Wars* and various religious/philosophical traditions. This section considered practical takeaways from these concepts.

If these takeaways resonate with readers, then it seems that the eighteen principles have merit. Perhaps they really are universal truths, applicable "for all time, all places and all people."[8]

CONCLUSION: "TRUTH ALONE TRIUMPHS"

Let's suppose that the eighteen principles discussed in this chapter are, in fact, universal truths. A question remains: How did people discover them? After all, a truth may exist and yet remain hidden, like a buried artifact.

Perhaps, in ancient times, some clever individual guessed the eighteen principles and shared them with a neighbor, who in turn shared them with another neighbor, and so on. However, given the lack of modern forms of communication, it seems unlikely that these principles could have spread throughout the world. Yet we find the eighteen concepts in ancient texts and traditions from a broad range of locations, including India, China, the Middle East, and the Americas. How can we explain this result?

The answer may lie in the following theory: Regarding the deepest principles of life, it is the nature of truth to reveal itself. In other words, the truth cannot be denied for long; sooner or later, it will come to light, no matter the time, location, or cultural context.

Many religious/philosophical traditions support this theory, as evidenced by the quotes below:

From the Upanishads: "Truth alone triumphs."[9]

From the Granth Sahib: "Falsehood will come to an end, O Nanak, and Truth will prevail in the end."[10]

From the Fourteenth Dalai Lama, a Tibetan Buddhist spiritual leader: "The power of truth never declines. Force and violence may be effective in the short term, but in the long run, it's the truth that prevails."[11]

From the Bible: "But when he, the Spirit of truth, comes, he will guide you into all the truth" (John 16:13 NIV).[12]

From the Koran: "The truth has come and the falsehood has vanished; surely falsehood is a vanishing (thing)."[13]

From a Vedic standpoint, life is like a river carrying us toward an ocean of truth. The closer we get to the ocean, the greater our joy and fulfillment will be. However, as human beings, we can choose whether to paddle with the current or against it. We can align ourselves with truth and righteousness or undermine these values through our words and actions.

It is clear what George Lucas would want. Based on the *Star Wars* films, he would prompt us to search our feelings and discover the truth. He would urge us to fulfill our destiny by supporting righteousness and resisting evil. In these ways, he would challenge us to follow in the footsteps of Luke Skywalker, the redeemed Anakin Skywalker, and Rey.

So, let's rise to the occasion. Let's pursue truth and virtue, striving to reach our full potential as human beings. By doing so, we will embody the wisdom of the Jedi.

APPENDIX A

Different Styles of Meditation

Having read the previous chapters, one may feel inspired to start meditating or return to a prior meditation practice. One may find it helpful to know that different styles of meditation have different effects on the brain. We can separate these styles into three categories—focused attention, open monitoring, and automatic self-transcending—based on the brainwaves they produce. Here is a brief overview of each category.

To quote scientists Frederick Travis and Jonathan Shear, "In *focused attention* or concentrative styles of meditations, voluntary sustained attention is focused on a given object, and attention is brought back to the object of attention when the mind has wandered."[1] Meditations in this category produce gamma and beta brainwaves; examples include Zen (third ventricle) and compassion meditation.

"*Open monitoring* or mindfulness-based meditations, involve the non-reactive monitoring of the content of ongoing experience, primarily as a means to become reflectively aware of the nature of emotional and cognitive patterns."[2] Meditations in this category produce theta brainwaves; examples include Vipassana and Kriya Yoga.

"*Automatic self-transcending* practices involve transcending of the procedures of the meditation. Since cognitive control increases mental activity, self-transcending procedures would need to involve minimal cognitive control—be automatic or effortless."[3] Meditations in this category produce alpha brainwaves; one example is the Transcendental Meditation technique. (The same brainwaves were also reported in a forty-five-year case study of a Qigong master.)

Thus, as stated earlier, different styles of meditation have different effects on the brain. So, what style should one practice? That depends on the results one is trying to achieve. To make an informed decision, one should research the scientifically verified benefits of various techniques (see appendix B).

APPENDIX B

Scientific Studies

One may be curious to learn more about the scientific studies on the state of yoga (see the "*Brahman*: Beyond the Physical Senses" section in chapter 2), mind-to-mind effects (see the "Mind-to-Mind Effects: 'The Force Is Strong with This One!'" section in chapter 5), and different styles of meditation (see appendix A). A few of these studies are listed below.

SCIENTIFIC STUDIES ON THE STATE OF YOGA BOTH AS A TEMPORARY EXPERIENCE AND AS A PERMANENT REALITY OF LIFE

Mason, L. I., C. N. Alexander, F. T. Travis, G. March, D. W. Orme-Johnson, J. Gackenbach, D. C. Mason, M. Rainforth, and K. G. Walton. "Electrophysiological Correlates of Higher States of Consciousness during Sleep in Long-Term Practitioners of the Transcendental Meditation Program." *Sleep* 20, no. 2 (February 1997): 102–10. https://pubmed.ncbi.nlm.nih.gov/9143069/.

Travis, Frederick. "Transcendental Experiences during Meditation Practice." *Annals of the New York Academy of Sciences* 1307 (January 2014): 1–8. https://pubmed.ncbi.nlm.nih.gov/24673148/.

Travis, Frederick, Alarik Arenander, and David DuBois. "Psychological and Physiological Characteristics of a Proposed Object-Referral/Self-Referral Continuum of Self-Awareness." *Consciousness and Cognition* 13, no. 2 (April 2004): 401–20. https://pubmed.ncbi.nlm.nih.gov/15134768/.

Travis, Frederick, and Craig Pearson. "Pure Consciousness: Distinct Phenomenological and Physiological Correlates of 'Consciousness Itself.'" *International Journal of*

Neuroscience 100, nos. 1–4 (February 2000): 77–89. https://pubmed.ncbi.nlm.nih
.gov/10512549/.

Travis, Frederick, Joe Tecce, Alarik Arenander, R. Keith Wallace. "Patterns of
EEG Coherence, Power, and Contingent Negative Variation Characterize the
Integration of Transcendental and Waking States." *Biological Psychology* 61, no. 3
(November 2002): 293–319. https://pubmed.ncbi.nlm.nih.gov/12406612/.

TWO KEY STUDIES ON MIND-TO-MIND EFFECTS

Kleinschnitz, Kurt Warren. "An Investigation into Field Effects of Consciousness
from the Perspectives of Maharishi's Vedic Science and Physics." PhD diss.,
Maharishi International University, 1997. https://www.proquest.com/docview
/304404768.

Travis, Frederick, and David Orme-Johnson. "Field Model of Consciousness: EEG
Coherence Changes as Indicators of Field Effects." *International Journal of
Neuroscience* 49, nos. 3–4 (December 1989): 203–11. https://pubmed.ncbi.nlm
.nih.gov/2700478/.

A KEY STUDY ON DIFFERENT
STYLES OF MEDITATION

Travis, Frederick, and Jonathan Shear. "Focused Attention, Open Monitoring and
Automatic Self-Transcending: Categories to Organize Meditations from Vedic,
Buddhist and Chinese Traditions." *Consciousness and Cognition* 19, no. 4 (February
2010): 1110–18. https://pubmed.ncbi.nlm.nih.gov/20167507/.

NOTES

CHAPTER 1

1. "Movie Franchises," The Numbers, accessed February 22, 2024, https://www.the-numbers.com/movies/franchises.

2. Rachel Swatman, "1977: Highest-Grossing Sci-Fi Series at the Box Office," Guinness World Records, August 19, 2015, https://www.guinnessworldrecords.com/news/60at60/2015/8/1977-highest-grossing-sci-fi-series-at-the-box-office-392957/.

3. Swatman, "1977."

4. Thomas Egenes, introduction to *The Upanishads: A New Translation*, trans. Vernon Katz and Thomas Egenes (New York: Jeremy P. Tarcher/Penguin, 2015), 3.

5. Michael Kaminski, *The Secret History of* Star Wars: *The Art of Storytelling and the Making of a Modern Epic* (Ontario: Legacy Books Press, 2008), 75–76.

6. George Lucas, "The Star Wars—From the Adventures of Luke Starkiller—Third Draft," Starkiller, March 31, 2010, https://www.starwarz.com/starkiller/the-star-wars-from-the-adventures-of-luke-starkiller-third-draft/.

7. George Lucas, "Star Wars (Public Version of Fourth Draft)," Starkiller, March 31, 2010, https://www.starwarz.com/starkiller/star-wars-public-version-of-fourth-draft/. Originally published in *The Art of Star Wars*, ed. Carol Titelman (New York: Ballantine Books, 1979).

8. Kaminski, *Secret History*, 78.

9. Kaminski, *Secret History*, 78.

10. Kaminski, *Secret History*, 76. See also Chris Taylor, *How* Star Wars *Conquered the Universe: The Past, Present, and Future of a Multibillion Dollar Franchise* (New York: Basic Books, 2014), 59.

11. "The Religious Affiliation of Director George Lucas," Adherents, May 27, 2005, https://web.archive.org/web/20050612235541/http:/www.adherents.com/people/pl/George_Lucas.html.

12. Transcendental Meditation, TM-Sidhi, Consciousness-Based, Maharishi Vedic Science, and Maharishi International University are registered or common law trademarks used under sublicense or with permission.

13. Irina Aleksander, "Look Who's Meditating Now," *New York Times*, March 18, 2011, https://www.nytimes.com/2011/03/20/fashion/20TM.html.

14. Evidently, George Lucas has continued to value the Transcendental Meditation technique, backing Operation Warrior Wellness, an initiative that teaches this technique to veterans suffering from post-traumatic stress disorder (PTSD). "Filmmaker Introduces Veterans to Meditation," *Wall Street Journal*, updated November 26, 2010, https://www.wsj.com/articles/SB10001424052748704638304575636911988306800.

It is also noteworthy that the George Lucas Educational Foundation website includes an article on the benefits of Transcendental Meditation practice in schools. "How Daily Meditation Improves Behavior," Edutopia, February 23, 2012, https://www.edutopia.org/stw-student-stress-meditation-overview-video.

15. Aleksander, "Look Who's Meditating Now." See also Leslie Tamura, "The Key to David Lynch's Happy Life," *Washington Post*, June 20, 2011, https://www.washingtonpost.com/national/the-key-to-david-lynchs-happy-life/2011/06/10/AGmR8NdH_story.html.

16. Cited in J. W. Rinzler, *The Making of* Star Wars (New York: Ballantine Books, 2007), 18; emphasis added.

17. Cited in Ryder Windham, Star Wars Episode I: The Phantom Menace *Movie Scrapbook* (New York: Random House, 1999), 13.

18. George Lucas, "The Mythology of 'Star Wars' with George Lucas," interview by Bill Moyers, BillMoyers.com, June 18, 1999, https://billmoyers.com/content/mythology-of-star-wars-george-lucas/.

19. See Mount Madonna School Values in World Thought, "George Lucas: Project Happiness Interview," YouTube, July 19, 2016, video, 15:17–18:01, https://www.youtube.com/watch?v=2TdGd0MlmvI&t=1014s.

20. Mount Madonna School, "George Lucas," 15:17–18:01.

21. Stephen Larsen and Robin Larsen, *Joseph Campbell: A Fire in the Mind—The Authorized Biography* (Rochester, VT: Inner Traditions, 2002), 540–43.

22. Larsen and Larsen, *Joseph Campbell*, 540–43.

23. Although the Vedas have been referred to as Hindu scripture, they predate Hinduism. *Boundless World History* elaborates on the origins of Hinduism: "Western scholars regard Hinduism as a synthesis, or fusion, of various Indian cultures and traditions, with diverse roots and no stated founder. This synthesis is believed to have developed after Vedic times, between 500 BCE and 300 CE." Boundless, "The Rise of Hinduism," in *Boundless World History*, ed. Lumen Learning (New York: State University of New York OER Services, 2018), https://courses.lumenlearning.com/suny-hccc-worldcivilization/chapter/the-rise-of-hinduism/.

24. Egenes, introduction, 3–6.

25. Cited in Maurice Bloomfield, *The Religion of the Veda: The Ancient Religion of India (From Rig-Veda to Upanishads)* (New York: G. P. Putnam's Sons, 1908), 55. Also cited in Egenes, introduction, 4.

26. Om Prie Srivastava, introduction to *Bhagavad Gita: The Art and Science of Management for the 21st Century* (India: Zorba Books, 2018), 9–10. See also James A. Hijiya, "The *Gita* of J. Robert Oppenheimer," *Proceedings of the American Philosophical Society* 144, no. 2 (June 2000): 130.

27. Mahatma Gandhi, "Mahatma Gandhi's Address to Missionaries," *The Missionary Review of the World* 49, no. 1 (January 1926): 35.

28. Egenes, introduction, 3.

29. Maharishi Mahesh Yogi, trans., "Rig-Veda 1.164.46," in *Human Physiology: Expression of Veda and the Vedic Literature*, by Tony Nader (Fairfield, IA: Maharishi International University Press, 2015), 514.

30. Windham, *Movie Scrapbook*, 13.

31. George Lucas, dir., *Star Wars: Episode IV—A New Hope*, written by George Lucas (1977; San Francisco: Lucasfilm, 2019), DVD.

32. Irvin Kershner, dir., *Star Wars: Episode V—The Empire Strikes Back*, screenplay by Leigh Brackett and Lawrence Kasdan, story by George Lucas (1980; San Francisco: Lucasfilm, 2019), DVD.

33. Richard Marquand, dir., *Star Wars: Episode VI—Return of the Jedi*, screenplay by Lawrence Kasdan and George Lucas, story by George Lucas (1983; San Francisco: Lucasfilm, 2019), DVD.

34. George Lucas, dir., *Star Wars: Episode I—The Phantom Menace*, written by George Lucas (1999; San Francisco: Lucasfilm, 2019), DVD.

35. George Lucas, dir., *Star Wars: Episode II—Attack of the Clones*, screenplay by George Lucas and Jonathan Hales (2002; San Francisco: Lucasfilm, 2019), DVD.

36. George Lucas, dir., *Star Wars: Episode III—Revenge of the Sith*, written by George Lucas (2005; San Francisco: Lucasfilm, 2019), DVD.

37. J. J. Abrams, dir., *Star Wars: Episode VII—The Force Awakens*, written by Lawrence Kasdan, J. J. Abrams, and Michael Arndt; based on characters by George Lucas (2015; San Francisco: Lucasfilm and Bad Robot Productions, 2019), DVD.

38. Rian Johnson, dir., *Star Wars: Episode VIII—The Last Jedi*, written by Rian Johnson, based on characters by George Lucas (2017; San Francisco: Lucasfilm, 2019), DVD.

39. J. J. Abrams, dir., *Star Wars: Episode IX—The Rise of Skywalker*, screenplay by Chris Terrio and J. J. Abrams; story by Derek Connolly, Colin Trevorrow, J. J. Abrams, and Chris Terrio; based on characters by George Lucas (2019; San Francisco: Lucasfilm and Bad Robot Productions, 2020), DVD.

CHAPTER 2

1. George Lucas, screenplay of *Star Wars: Episode IV—A New Hope*, in Star Wars*: The Annotated Screenplays*, annotated by Laurent Bouzereau (New York: Ballantine Books, 1997), 89.

2. "100 Greatest Movie Quotes of All Time," American Film Institute, accessed February 22, 2024, https://www.afi.com/afis-100-years-100-movie-quotes/; "Hollywood's 100 Favorite Movie Quotes," *Hollywood Reporter*, February 24, 2016, https://www.hollywoodreporter.com/lists/best-movie-quotes-hollywoods-top-867142/.

3. "List of References to *Star Wars* in Television," *Star Wars* Fanpedia, accessed February 22, 2024, https://starwarsfans.fandom.com/wiki/List_of_references_to_Star_Wars_in_television. See also "List of References to *Star Wars* in Movies," *Star Wars* Fanpedia, accessed February 22, 2024, https://starwarsfans.fandom.com/wiki/List_of_references_to_Star_Wars_in_movies.

4. Dawn Yanek, "May the 4th Be with You: All about the *Star Wars* Holiday," *Reader's Digest*, April 29, 2022, https://www.rd.com/article/may-the-fourth-star-wars-holiday/. To quote this source, "The California legislature voted in 2019 to officially turn May 4th into *Star Wars* Day."

5. Rian Johnson, dir., *Star Wars: Episode VIII—The Last Jedi*, written by Rian Johnson, based on characters by George Lucas (San Francisco: Lucasfilm, 2019), DVD, 0:48:07–0:48:21.

6. Swami Lokeswarananda, trans., *Chandogya Upanishad* (Kolkata, India: Ramakrishna Mission Institute of Culture, 2017), verses 6.13.1–3, updated March 14, 2019, https://www.wisdomlib.org/hinduism/book/chandogya-upanishad-english.

7. Vernon Katz and Thomas Egenes, trans., "Mundaka Upanishad 1.1.6," in *The Upanishads: A New Translation* (New York: Jeremy P. Tarcher/Penguin, 2015), 88–89.

8. Johnson, *The Last Jedi*, 0:48:07–0:48:21.

9. Lucas, screenplay of *A New Hope*, 59.

10. Lucas, screenplay of *A New Hope*, 115.

11. Maharishi Mahesh Yogi, trans., "Bhagavad Gita 2.67," in *Maharishi Mahesh Yogi on the Bhagavad-Gita: A New Translation and Commentary with Sanskrit Text* (Fairfield, IA: Maharishi International University Press, 2015), 167. The Bhagavad Gita often uses masculine nouns and pronouns (such as "man," "he," and "him"); nonetheless, the teachings of this text are thought to apply to all people regardless of gender. The same goes for the other texts discussed in this book.

12. Thomas Egenes, trans., "Yoga Sutra 1.2," in *Maharishi Patañjali Yoga Sūtra* (Fairfield, IA: 1st World Publishing, 2010), 11.

13. K. Narayanasvami Aiyar, trans., "Tejobindu Upanishad of Krishna-yajurveda, Chapter III," in *Thirty Minor Upaniṣads*, ed. Madhu Khanna (New Delhi: Tantra Foundation, 2011), updated July 2, 2023, https://www.wisdomlib.org/hinduism/book/thirty-minor-upanishads/. In this source, *sat chit ananda* is transliterated as "Saccidananda."

14. Ravi Shankar, "Chapter 11: The Six Distortions of Love," in *Wisdom for the New Millennium* (Mumbai, India: Aslan Reads, 2019), 95.

15. See "Yoga Sutra 1.3" in Egenes, *Maharishi Patañjali Yoga Sūtra*, 12.

16. Maharishi Mahesh Yogi, trans., "Nrisimhottaratapaniya Upanishad 1," in *Ramayan in Human Physiology*, by Tony Nader (Fairfield, IA: Maharishi International University Press, 2011), 19.

17. Egenes, "Yoga Sutra 1.2," in *Maharishi Patañjali Yoga Sūtra*, 11.

18. Frederick Travis, "Transcendental Experiences during Meditation Practice," *Annals of the New York Academy of Sciences* 1307 (January 2014): 1–8; Maharishi, *On the Bhagavad-Gita*, 210; Frederick Travis and Jonathan Shear, "Focused Attention, Open Monitoring and Automatic Self-Transcending: Categories to Organize Meditations from Vedic, Buddhist and Chinese Traditions," *Consciousness and Cognition* 19, no. 4 (February 2010): 1110–18.

19. Maharishi, *On the Bhagavad-Gita*, 313.

20. Frederick Travis and Craig Pearson, "Pure Consciousness: Distinct Phenomenological and Physiological Correlates of 'Consciousness Itself,'" *International Journal of Neuroscience* 100, nos. 1–4 (February 2000): 77.

21. Travis, "Transcendental Experiences," 1.

22. Travis, "Transcendental Experiences," 4; Maharishi, *On the Bhagavad-Gita*, 313.

23. Egenes, "Yoga Sutra 1.14," in *Maharishi Patañjali Yoga Sūtra*, 17.

24. Maharishi, *On the Bhagavad-Gita*, 135.

25. Travis, "Transcendental Experiences," 1.

26. Travis, "Transcendental Experiences," 1.

27. Travis, "Transcendental Experiences," 1.

28. Travis, "Transcendental Experiences," 1.

29. Maharishi Mahesh Yogi, *Constitution of India Fulfilled through Maharishi's Transcendental Meditation* (India: Age of Enlightenment Publications, 1999), 65.

30. Maharishi, "Bhagavad Gita 6.29," in *On the Bhagavad-Gita*, 441.

31. Maharishi, *On the Bhagavad-Gita*, 313.

32. In this book, the word "evolutionary" refers to not merely Darwinian evolution but also progressive development in every sphere of life—which culminates in higher states of human awareness.

33. Lucas, screenplay of *A New Hope*, 118.

34. Leigh Brackett and Lawrence Kasdan, screenplay of *Star Wars: Episode V—The Empire Strikes Back*, in Bouzereau, *Annotated Screenplays*, 187.

35. Brackett and Kasdan, screenplay of *The Empire Strikes Back*, 187.

36. Egenes, "Yoga Sutra," in *Maharishi Patañjali Yoga Sūtra*, 73–106.

37. Cine Extras, "Deleted Scenes—Yoda Communes with Qui-Gon—*Star Wars Episode III Revenge of the Sith* 2005," YouTube, May 12, 2020, video, 12:54–13:51, https://www.youtube.com/watch?v=BnMWRkCkEks.

38. Johnson, *The Last Jedi*, 0:48:59–0:50:01.

CHAPTER 3

1. Rian Johnson, dir., *Star Wars: Episode VIII—The Last Jedi*, written by Rian Johnson, based on characters by George Lucas (San Francisco: Lucasfilm, 2019), DVD, 0:48:07–0:48:21.

2. Johnson, *The Last Jedi*, 0:48:59–0:50:01.

3. Johnson, *The Last Jedi*, 0:48:59–0:50:01.

4. Vernon Katz, trans., "Bhagavad Gita 14.11–14.13," in *Bhagavad-Gita: All 18 Chapters*, trans. Maharishi Mahesh Yogi and Vernon Katz (Fairfield, IA: Department of Maharishi Vedic Science, Maharishi International University, n.d.), electronic file, 81.

5. Johnson, *The Last Jedi*, 0:48:07–0:48:21.

6. Cited in Ryder Windham, Star Wars Episode I: The Phantom Menace *Movie Scrapbook* (New York: Random House, 1999), 13.

7. Maharishi Mahesh Yogi, trans., "Bhagavad Gita 3.36–37," in *Maharishi Mahesh Yogi on the Bhagavad-Gita: A New Translation and Commentary with Sanskrit Text* (Fairfield, IA: Maharishi International University Press, 2015), 235–36. "Varshneya" refers to Sri Krishna's family and clan. *Rajo-guna* is another term for *rajas*.

8. Maharishi, *On the Bhagavad-Gita*, 237.

9. Maharishi, *On the Bhagavad-Gita*, 236.

10. Maharishi, "Brihadaranyaka Upanishad 1.4.2," in *On the Bhagavad-Gita*, 50.

11. Maharishi, "Bhagavad Gita 2.18," in *On the Bhagavad-Gita*, 97.

12. Maharishi, "Bhagavad Gita 2.23," in *On the Bhagavad-Gita*, 101.

13. Maharishi, "Bhagavad Gita 2.40," in *On the Bhagavad-Gita*, 117.

14. Maharishi, "Bhagavad Gita 1.23," in *On the Bhagavad-Gita*, 44; emphasis added.

15. Leigh Brackett and Lawrence Kasdan, screenplay of *Star Wars: Episode V—The Empire Strikes Back*, in Star Wars: *The Annotated Screenplays*, annotated by Laurent Bouzereau (New York: Ballantine Books, 1997), 180.

CHAPTER 4

1. Bill Kroyer, dir., *FernGully: The Last Rainforest*, screenplay by Jim Cox, original stories by Diana Young (N.p.: FAI Films, Interscope Communications, Kroyer Films, and Youngheart Productions, 1992), 0:07:24–0:07:49.

2. Rian Johnson, dir., *Star Wars: Episode VIII—The Last Jedi*, written by Rian Johnson, based on characters by George Lucas (San Francisco: Lucasfilm, 2019), DVD, 0:48:07–0:48:21.

3. Johnson, *The Last Jedi*, 0:48:59–0:50:01.

4. Maharishi Mahesh Yogi, *Maharishi Mahesh Yogi on the Bhagavad-Gita: A New Translation and Commentary with Sanskrit Text* (Fairfield, IA: Maharishi International University Press, 2015), 27.

5. Maharishi, *On the Bhagavad*-Gita, 26–27.

6. Maharishi, *On the Bhagavad-Gita*, 26–27.

7. Maharishi, *On the Bhagavad-Gita*, 27.

8. Maharishi, *On the Bhagavad-Gita*, 64.

9. George Lucas, dir., *Star Wars: Episode I—The Phantom Menace*, written by George Lucas (San Francisco: Lucasfilm, 2019), DVD, 1:25:21–1:25:26.

10. J. J. Abrams, dir., *Star Wars: Episode VII—The Force Awakens*, written by Lawrence Kasdan, J. J. Abrams, and Michael Arndt, based on characters by George Lucas (San Francisco: Lucasfilm and Bad Robot Productions, 2019), DVD, 0:02:51–0:03:09.

11. Maharishi, "Bhagavad Gita 4.7–8," in *On the Bhagavad-Gita*, 262–63. In this quote, "Bharata" refers to Arjuna, who is a descendant of the great king Bharata.

12. Johnson, *The Last Jedi*, 0:48:07–0:48:21.

13. K. Krishna Murthy, "Dharma—Its Etymology," *The Tibet Journal* 21, no. 1 (Spring 1996): 84.

14. M. Monier-Williams, *A Sanskrit-English Dictionary: Etymologically and Philologically Arranged with Special Reference to Cognate Indo-European Languages* (Oxford: Clarendon Press, 1899), updated May 31, 2022, https://www.wisdomlib.org/definition/dhri.

15. Ram Dass, *Be Here Now* (New York: HarperCollins, 2010), Kindle, 54.

16. S. Radhakrishnan, "Bhagavad Gita 18.43," in *The Bhagavadgita* (New York: HarperCollins, 2010), 433.

17. Maharishi, "Bhagavad Gita 3.8," in *On the Bhagavad-Gita*, 191.

18. See Maharishi, *On the Bhagavad-Gita*, for a detailed discussion of Sri Krishna's arguments.

19. Maharishi, "Bhagavad Gita 2.31," in *On the Bhagavad-Gita*, 108.

20. Lucas, *The Phantom Menace*, 1:25:21–1:25:26.

CHAPTER 5

1. Roger Allers and Rob Minkoff, dirs., *The Lion King*, screenplay by Irene Mecchi, Jonathan Roberts, and Linda Woolverton (Burbank, CA: Walt Disney Pictures and Walt Disney Feature Animation, 1994), 0:09:41–0:10:11.

2. See BarbaRossa, "We Are All Connected—Neil deGrasse Tyson," YouTube, November 12, 2010, video, 1:04, https://www.youtube.com/watch?v=CtWB90bVUO8.

3. Swami Lokeswarananda, trans., *Chandogya Upanishad* (Kolkata, India: Ramakrishna Mission Institute of Culture, 2017), verses 6.13.1–3, updated March 14, 2019, https://www.wisdomlib.org/hinduism/book/chandogya-upanishad-english.

4. "Being Love," Ram Dass, accessed February 22, 2024, https://www.ramdass.org/being-love/.

5. Frederick Travis and David Orme-Johnson, "Field Model of Consciousness: EEG Coherence Changes as Indicators of Field Effects," *International Journal of Neuroscience* 49, nos. 3–4 (December 1989): 203–11.

6. Kurt Warren Kleinschnitz, "An Investigation into Field Effects of Consciousness from the Perspectives of Maharishi's Vedic Science and Physics" (PhD diss., Maharishi International University, 1997), https://www.proquest.com/docview/304404768.

7. George Lucas, screenplay of *Star Wars: Episode IV—A New Hope*, in Star Wars: *The Annotated Screenplays*, annotated by Laurent Bouzereau (New York: Ballantine Books, 1997), 70.

8. Lucas, screenplay of *A New Hope*, 115.

9. Chris Terrio quoted in *The Skywalker Legacy: The Making of* Star Wars: Episode IX—The Rise of Skywalker *(2019)*, directed by Debs Paterson (San Francisco: Lucasfilm, 2020), DVD. Quote also cited in "Force Dyad," Wookieepedia, accessed February 22, 2024, https://starwars.fandom.com/wiki/Force_dyad.

10. Thomas Egenes, trans., "Yoga Sutra 3.16," in *Maharishi Patañjali Yoga Sūtra* (Fairfield, IA: 1st World Publishing, 2010), 83.

11. Collective consciousness can also be *rajasic*, meaning energetic and impassioned, though that topic is not as relevant to this section. For information about the Vedic principles of *sattva*, *rajas*, and *tamas*, see "Balance and Imbalance, *Dharma* and *Adharma*" in chapter 4.

12. Lucas, screenplay of *A New Hope*, 58.

13. J. J. Abrams, dir., *Star Wars: Episode IX—The Rise of Skywalker*, screenplay by Chris Terrio and J. J. Abrams; story by Derek Connolly, Colin Trevorrow, J. J. Abrams, and Chris Terrio; based on characters by George Lucas (San Francisco: Lucasfilm and Bad Robot Productions, 2020), DVD, 1:45:03–1:45:26.

14. Abrams, *The Rise of Skywalker*, 1:57:22–1:57:41.

15. Abrams, *The Rise of Skywalker*, 1:57:41–1:58:34.

16. Abrams, *The Rise of Skywalker*, 0:10:31–0:10:41.

17. Abrams, *The Rise of Skywalker*, 1:59:13–1:59:28.

18. Abrams, *The Rise of Skywalker*, 1:59:28–1:59:42.

CHAPTER 6

1. Kate Golembiewski, "Life after Death? Cryonicists Try to Defy Mortality by Freezing Bodies," *Discover Magazine*, October 14, 2022, https://www.discovermagazine.com/technology/will-cryonically-frozen-bodies-ever-be-brought-back-to-life.

2. George Lucas, dir., *Star Wars: Episode III—Revenge of the Sith*, written by George Lucas (San Francisco: Lucasfilm, 2019), DVD, 0:33:27–0:34:41.

3. Lawrence Kasdan and George Lucas, screenplay of *Star Wars: Episode VI—Return of the Jedi*, in Star Wars: *The Annotated Screenplays*, annotated by Laurent Bouzereau (New York: Ballantine Books, 1997), 266.

4. Kasdan and Lucas, screenplay of *Return of the Jedi*, 266.

5. Maharishi Mahesh Yogi, trans., "Bhagavad Gita 2.27," in *Maharishi Mahesh Yogi on the Bhagavad-Gita: A New Translation and Commentary with Sanskrit Text* (Fairfield, IA: Maharishi International University Press, 2015), 104.

6. Maharishi, "Bhagavad Gita 2.34," in *On the Bhagavad-Gita*, 110.

7. Jonathan Nolan and Christopher Nolan, "*The Dark Knight*: 2008 Film," Script Slug, accessed February 22, 2024, https://www.scriptslug.com/script/the-dark-knight-2008.

8. Lucas, *Revenge of the Sith*, 0:33:27–0:34:41.

9. Lucas, *Revenge of the Sith*, 0:33:27–0:34:41.

10. Lucas, *Revenge of the Sith*, 0:46:00–0:48:00.

11. Lucas, *Revenge of the Sith*, 0:33:27–0:34:41.

12. Lucas, *Revenge of the Sith*, 0:33:27–0:34:41.

13. Cine Extras, "Deleted Scenes—Yoda Communes with Qui-Gon—*Star Wars Episode III Revenge of the Sith* 2005," YouTube, May 12, 2020, video, 12:54–13:51, https://www.youtube.com/watch?v=BnMWRkCkEks.

14. Cine Extras, "Yoda Communes," 12:54–13:51.

15. George Lucas, screenplay of *Star Wars: Episode IV—A New Hope*, in Bouzereau, *Annotated Screenplays*, 80.

16. Lucas, screenplay of *A New Hope*, 80.

17. Lucas, screenplay of *A New Hope*, 81.

18. Lucas, screenplay of *A New Hope*, 115.

19. Maharishi, "Bhagavad Gita 2.18," in *On the Bhagavad-Gita*, 97.

20. Maharishi, "Bhagavad Gita 2.22," in *On the Bhagavad-Gita*, 100.

21. Maharishi, "Bhagavad Gita 2.13," in *On the Bhagavad-Gita*, 92.

22. Maharishi Mahesh Yogi, trans., "Brihadaranyaka Upanishad 1.3.28," in "Vedic Expressions Used in Maharishi Vedic Science" (Fairfield, IA: Department of Maharishi Vedic Science, Maharishi International University, n.d.), electronic file, 45. Technically, the pronoun in this verse should be translated as "me," not "us." Otherwise, this translation is satisfactory.

23. Vernon Katz and Thomas Egenes, trans., "Isha Upanishad 17," in *The Upanishads: A New Translation* (New York: Jeremy P. Tarcher/Penguin, 2015), 32.

24. "Oneness," Wookieepedia, accessed February 22, 2024, https://starwars.fandom.com/wiki/Oneness.

CHAPTER 7

1. "'You've Got to Find What You Love,' Jobs Says," *Stanford News*, June 12, 2005, https://news.stanford.edu/2005/06/12/youve-got-find-love-jobs-says/.

2. George Lucas, screenplay of *Star Wars: Episode IV—A New Hope*, in Star Wars: The Annotated Screenplays, annotated by Laurent Bouzereau (New York: Ballantine Books, 1997), 59.

3. Lucas, screenplay of *A New Hope*, 59.

4. Lucas, screenplay of *A New Hope*, 59.

5. "Newton's Third Law," Physics Classroom, accessed February 22, 2024, https://www.physicsclassroom.com/class/newtlaws/Lesson-4/Newton-s-Third-Law.

6. Lucas, screenplay of *A New Hope*, 59.

7. Sadhguru, "The Eternal Outlaw," in *Adiyogi: The Source of Yoga*, by Sadhguru and Arundhathi Subramaniam (New York: HarperCollins, 2017), 39.

8. Thomas Egenes, trans., "Yoga Sutra 3.22," in *Maharishi Patañjali Yoga Sūtra* (Fairfield, IA: 1st World Publishing, 2010), 87.

9. Lucas, screenplay of *A New Hope*, 59.

10. Leigh Brackett and Lawrence Kasdan, screenplay of *Star Wars: Episode V—The Empire Strikes Back*, in Bouzereau, *Annotated Screenplays*, 180.

11. Brackett and Kasdan, screenplay of *The Empire Strikes Back*, 180.

CHAPTER 8

1. "'You've Got to Find What You Love,' Jobs Says," *Stanford News*, June 12, 2005, https://news.stanford.edu/2005/06/12/youve-got-find-love-jobs-says/.

2. George Lucas, screenplay of *Star Wars: Episode IV—A New Hope*, in Star Wars: *The Annotated Screenplays*, annotated by Laurent Bouzereau (New York: Ballantine Books, 1997), 61.

3. These lines do not appear in the original 1980 version of *The Empire Strikes Back*; they were added later in a special edition of the film. *Star Wars* Comparison, "Original Emperor's Message—*The Empire Strikes Back* (1980)," YouTube, October 10, 2016, video, 1:19, https://www.youtube.com/watch?v=tzUg74pcvc8.

4. Leigh Brackett and Lawrence Kasdan, screenplay of *Star Wars: Episode V—The Empire Strikes Back*, in Bouzereau, *Annotated Screenplays*, 216.

5. Lawrence Kasdan and George Lucas, screenplay of *Star Wars: Episode VI—Return of the Jedi*, in Bouzereau, *Annotated Screenplays*, 292.

6. Kasdan and Lucas, screenplay of *Return of the Jedi*, 290.

7. Thomas Egenes, trans., "Yoga Sutra 1.48," in *Maharishi Patañjali Yoga Sūtra* (Fairfield, IA: 1st World Publishing, 2010), 37.

8. Sadhguru, *Of Mystics and Mistakes* (Ahmedabad: Jaico Publishing House, 2012), 135.

9. Egenes, "Yoga Sutra 3.33," in *Maharishi Patañjali Yoga Sūtra*, 92.

10. George Lucas, dir., *Star Wars: Episode III—Revenge of the Sith*, written by George Lucas (San Francisco: Lucasfilm, 2019), DVD, 0:33:27–0:34:41.

11. See Egenes, "Yoga Sutra 2.3," in *Maharishi Patañjali Yoga Sūtra*, 44.

12. "Jealous," in *New Oxford American Dictionary*, 3rd ed. (New York: Oxford University Press, 2010).

13. "Greed" in *New Oxford American Dictionary*.

14. Lucas, *Revenge of the Sith*, 0:33:27–0:34:41.

15. Lucas, screenplay of *A New Hope*, 59; emphasis added.

16. Lucas, screenplay of *A New Hope*, 115.
17. Lucas, screenplay of *A New Hope*, 115.
18. Lucas, screenplay of *A New Hope*, 118.
19. Kasdan and Lucas, screenplay of *Return of the Jedi*, 292; emphasis added.
20. Egenes, "Yoga Sutra 2.3," in *Maharishi Patañjali Yoga Sūtra*, 44.
21. Egenes, "Yoga Sutra 1.30," in *Maharishi Patañjali Yoga Sūtra*, 26; emphasis added.
22. Maharishi Mahesh Yogi, trans., "Bhagavad Gita 3.25," in *Maharishi Mahesh Yogi on the Bhagavad-Gita: A New Translation and Commentary with Sanskrit Text* (Fairfield, IA: Maharishi International University Press, 2015), 217.
23. Maharishi, "Bhagavad Gita 2.38," in *On the Bhagavad-Gita*, 113.
24. Egenes, "Yoga Sutra 1.15," in *Maharishi Patañjali Yoga Sūtra*, 18.
25. Egenes, "Yoga Sutra 1.16," in *Maharishi Patañjali Yoga Sūtra*, 18.

CHAPTER 9

1. Gary Player, foreword to *How to Build a Classic Golf Swing*, by Ernie Els (New York: Harper Perennial, 1999), 6.
2. Cited in Scott Andrew, *The Rugged Entrepreneur: What Every Disruptive Business Leader Should Know* (New York: Forefront Books, 2021), 87.
3. George Lucas, screenplay of *Star Wars: Episode IV—A New Hope*, in *Star Wars: The Annotated Screenplays*, annotated by Laurent Bouzereau (New York: Ballantine Books, 1997), 42.
4. Lucas, screenplay of *A New Hope*, 42.
5. Maharishi Mahesh Yogi, trans., "Bhagavad Gita 2.38," in *Maharishi Mahesh Yogi on the Bhagavad-Gita: A New Translation and Commentary with Sanskrit Text* (Fairfield, IA: Maharishi International University Press, 2015), 113.
6. Maharishi, "Bhagavad 2.66," in *On the Bhagavad-Gita*, 165.
7. Thomas Egenes, trans., "Yoga Sutra 3.19," in *Maharishi Patañjali Yoga Sūtra* (Fairfield, IA: 1st World Publishing, 2010), 85.
8. Maharishi, "Bhagavad Gita 4.38," in *On the Bhagavad-Gita*, 311.
9. Leigh Brackett and Lawrence Kasdan, screenplay of *Star Wars: Episode V—The Empire Strikes Back*, in Bouzereau, *Annotated Screenplays*, 187.
10. Egenes, "Yoga Sutra 2.5," in *Maharishi Patañjali Yoga Sūtra*, 45.
11. Maharishi, "Bhagavad Gita 5.15," in *On the Bhagavad-Gita*, 354.
12. Maharishi, "Bhagavad Gita 5.16," in *On the Bhagavad-Gita*, 355.
13. Vernon Katz and Thomas Egenes, trans., "Shvetashvatara Upanishad 5.1," in *The Upanishads: A New Translation* (New York: Jeremy P. Tarcher/Penguin, 2015), 162.
14. Katz and Egenes, "Mundaka Upanishad 3.1.6," in *Upanishads*, 98.
15. Katz and Egenes, "Shvetashvatara Upanishad 6.13," in *Upanishads*, 168.
16. Maharishi, "Bhagavad Gita 6.8," in *On the Bhagavad-Gita*, 400.
17. Vernon Katz, trans., "Bhagavad Gita 7.2," in *Bhagavad-Gita: All 18 Chapters*, trans. Maharishi Mahesh Yogi and Vernon Katz (Fairfield, IA: Department of

Maharishi Vedic Science Department, Maharishi International University, n.d.), electronic file, 42.

18. Brackett and Kasdan, screenplay of *The Empire Strikes Back*, 187.

19. Rian Johnson, dir., *Star Wars: Episode VIII—The Last Jedi*, written by Rian Johnson, based on characters by George Lucas (San Francisco: Lucasfilm, 2019), DVD, 1:21:51–1:23:00.

20. Maharishi, "Bhagavad Gita 2.46," in *On the Bhagavad-Gita*, 132.

CHAPTER 10

1. Leigh Brackett and Lawrence Kasdan, screenplay of *Star Wars: Episode V—The Empire Strikes Back*, in Star Wars: *The Annotated Screenplays*, annotated by Laurent Bouzereau (New York: Ballantine Books, 1997), 187.

2. This quote is often attributed to Pierre Teilhard de Chardin; however, evidence suggests that it was actually written by Wayne W. Dyer. See "You Are Not a Human Being Having a Spiritual Experience. You Are a Spiritual Being Having a Human Experience," Quote Investigator, June 20, 2019, https://quoteinvestigator.com/2019/06/20/spiritual/.

3. Maharishi Mahesh Yogi, trans., "Bhagavad Gita 2.22," in *Maharishi Mahesh Yogi on the Bhagavad-Gita: A New Translation and Commentary with Sanskrit Text* (Fairfield, IA: Maharishi International University Press, 2015), 100.

4. Maharishi, "Bhagavad Gita 2.18," in *On the Bhagavad-Gita*, 97.

5. Thomas Egenes, trans., "Yoga Sutra 1.2–1.3," in *Maharishi Patañjali Yoga Sūtra* (Fairfield, IA: 1st World Publishing, 2010), 11–12.

6. Vernon Katz and Thomas Egenes, trans., "Katha Upanishad 1.3.15," in *The Upanishads: A New Translation* (New York: Jeremy P. Tarcher/Penguin, 2015), 58.

7. Katz and Egenes, "Mundaka Upanishad 2.2.8," in *Upanishads*, 96.

8. Katz and Egenes, "Katha Upanishad 2.2.13," in *Upanishads*, 65.

9. Brackett and Kasdan, screenplay of *The Empire Strikes Back*, 187.

10. Brackett and Kasdan, screenplay of *The Empire Strikes Back*, 188.

11. Maharishi Mahesh Yogi, trans., "Rig-Veda 1.89.8," in "Vedic Expressions Used in Maharishi Vedic Science" (Fairfield, IA: Department of Maharishi Vedic Science, Maharishi International University, n.d.), electronic file, 5.

12. Maharishi, "Upanishads of Krishna Yajur-Veda," introductory verse in "Vedic Expressions Used in Maharishi Vedic Science," 36.

13. Paramahansa Yogananda, *Sayings of Paramahansa Yogananda* (Los Angeles: Self-Realization Fellowship, 1986), 54.

14. George Lucas, dir., *Star Wars: Episode III—Revenge of the Sith*, written by George Lucas (San Francisco: Lucasfilm, 2019), DVD, 0:45:43–0:46:00.

15. Yogananda discusses the benefits of selflessness: "There is a magnet in your heart that will attract true friends. That magnet is unselfishness, thinking of others first. . . . When you learn to live for others, they will live for you." Cited in Larry

Chang, comp. and ed., *Wisdom for the Soul: Five Millennia of Prescriptions for Spiritual Healing* (Washington, DC: Gnosophia Publishers, 2006), 325.

16. Maharishi, "Bhagavad Gita 3.25," in *On the Bhagavad-Gita*, 217.

17. Maharishi Mahesh Yogi, *Constitution of India Fulfilled through Maharishi's Transcendental Meditation* (India: Age of Enlightenment Publications, 1999), 65.

18. Maharishi, "Bhagavad Gita 6.29," in *On the Bhagavad-Gita*, 441.

19. Maharishi, "Maha Upanishad 6.71, also Manusmriti 11.12.22," in *Constitution of India*, 352.

20. George Lucas, screenplay of *Star Wars: Episode IV—A New Hope*, in Bouzereau, *Annotated Screenplays*, 34.

21. Lawrence Kasdan and George Lucas, screenplay of *Star Wars: Episode VI—Return of the Jedi*, in Bouzereau, *Annotated Screenplays*, 292.

22. Maharishi, *Constitution of India*, 65.

23. Maharishi, "Bhagavad Gita 4.36," in *On the Bhagavad-Gita*, 308.

24. Cited in J. W. Rinzler, *The Making of* Star Wars (New York: Ballantine Books, 2007), 18.

25. Lucas, screenplay of *A New Hope*, 59.

CHAPTER 11

1. George Lucas, "The Mythology of 'Star Wars' with George Lucas," interview by Bill Moyers, BillMoyers.com, June 18, 1999, https://billmoyers.com/content/mythology-of-star-wars-george-lucas/.

2. Cited in Ryder Windham, Star Wars Episode I: The Phantom Menace *Movie Scrapbook* (New York: Random House, 1999), 13; emphasis added.

3. Bedagi (Big Thunder), "Hunting the Moose," in *The Indians' Book: An Offering by the American Indians of Indian Lore, Musical and Narrative, to Form a Record of the Songs and Legends of Their Race*, comp. and ed. Natalie Curtis (New York: Harper and Brothers, 1907), 11. Quote also cited (with different punctuation) in John Girard and JoAnn Girard, comps., *Sage Sayings: Inspiring Native American Passages for Leaders* (CreateSpace Independent Publishing Platform, 2014), 29.

4. J. H. McDonald, trans., *Tao Te Ching*, chap. 34, updated December 6, 2007, http://www.wright-house.com/religions/taoism/tao-te-ching.html.

5. McDonald, *Tao Te Ching*, chap. 14.

6. Cited in J. W. Rinzler, *The Making of* Star Wars (New York: Ballantine Books, 2007), 18.

7. Rian Johnson, dir., *Star Wars: Episode VIII—The Last Jedi*, written by Rian Johnson, based on characters by George Lucas (San Francisco: Lucasfilm, 2019), DVD, 0:48:07–0:48:21.

8. Ibn Arabi, *Fusus al-Hikam*, cited in Karen Armstrong, "Towards Interfaith Understanding," in *Faith, Identity, Cohesion: Building a Better Future*, ed. Jolene Jerard and Amanda Huan (Singapore: World Scientific Publishing, 2020), 40–41.

9. Sikhism is an Indian religious/philosophical tradition that originated around the end of the fifteenth century CE.

10. Sant Singh Khalsa, trans., "Sri Guru Granth Sahib English Translation," 782, accessed February 29, 2024, http://sikhs.org/english/eg_index.htm.

11. Johnson, *The Last Jedi*, 0:48:59–0:50:01.

12. Black Elk, *The Sacred Pipe: Black Elk's Account of the Seven Rites of the Oglala Sioux*, recorded and edited by Joseph Epes Brown (Oklahoma: University of Oklahoma Press, 2012), 115. Quote also cited (with slight variations) in Girard and Girard, *Sage Sayings*, 66.

13. McDonald, *Tao Te Ching*, chap. 28.

14. Emphasis added. This book has mainly quoted the New International Version (NIV) of the Bible because this version's language is accessible to modern readers. However, in a few cases, this book has quoted the New King James Version (NKJV) instead because it seems to provide a more accurate translation of certain verses. Scholar Craig Pearson comments on different translations of Luke 17:21: "Some later translations render the final line of this passage as 'The kingdom of God is among you' or 'in your midst.' Ilaria Ramelli, a professor at Catholic University of the Sacred Heart, in Milan, Italy, has meticulously analyzed the ancient Syriac texts as well as the Greek grammar for this passage and other Gospel passages, and she concludes that the proper translation is 'God's Kingdom is inside you.'" Craig Pearson, *The Supreme Awakening: Experiences of Enlightenment Throughout Time—and How You Can Cultivate Them* (Fairfield, IA: Maharishi International University Press, 2016), 517–18.

15. M. R. Bawa Muhaiyaddeen, *To Die Before Death: The Sufi Way of Life* (Philadelphia: Fellowship Press, 1997), 96.

16. Cited in Aksapada, comp., *The Analects of Rumi* (N.p.: n.p., n.d.), 33.

17. Khalsa, "Sri Guru Granth Sahib," 1141.

18. Yellow Lark, trans., "Prayer for Appreciation," in *The Treasury of American Prayer*, by James P. Moore Jr. (New York: Doubleday, 2008), 84.

19. Noel Knockwood, "The Seven Sacred Prayer," in *Science and the Management of Protected Areas: Proceedings of an International Conference Held at Acadia University, Nova Scotia, Canada, 14–19 May 1991*, ed. J. H. M. Willison, S. Bondrup-Nielsen, C. Drysdale, T. B. Herman, N. W. P. Munro, and T. L. Pollock (Amsterdam: Elsevier Science, 1992), xiii.

20. Cited in Girard and Girard, *Sage Sayings*, 41.

21. Inayat Khan, "Saum," in *The Heart of Sufism: Essential Writings of Hazrat Inayat Khan*, ed. H. J. Witteveen (Boston: Shambala Publications, 1999), 80.

22. Nanak, "Japji—The Morning Prayer," in *Japji: The Immortal Prayer-Chant*, trans. Khushwant Singh (New Delhi: Abhinav Publications, 1987), 11.

23. Takao Maruyama, "Buddha's Supernatural Powers in the Lotus Sutra" (paper presented at the 34th International Congress of Asian and North African Studies, Hong Kong, August 1993), 9.

24. "Theravada Buddhism," BBC, updated October 2, 2002, https://www.bbc.co
.uk/religion/religions/buddhism/subdivisions/theravada_1.shtml.

25. Zhuangzi, *The Complete Works of Zhuangzi*, trans. Burton Watson (New York: Columbia University Press, 2013), 3.

26. Liezi, "Book II: The Yellow Emperor," in *Taoist Teachings from the Book of Lieh Tzu*, trans. Lionel Giles (New York: E. P. Dutton, 1912), 47.

27. Sarah Winnemucca, "The Pah-Utes," *Californian* 6, no. 33 (September 1882): 252–56. Reprinted in *The Sagebrush Anthology: Literature from the Silver Age of the Old West*, ed. Lawrence I. Berkove (Columbia: University of Missouri Press, 2006), 331.

28. Cited in Michael Oren Fitzgerald and Judith Fitzgerald, eds., *Indian Spirit* (Bloomington, IN: World Wisdom, 2006), 125.

29. Annemarie Schimmel, "Islam: Tales and Legends Concerning Religious Figures," Encyclopedia Britannica, accessed February 22, 2024, https://www.britannica.com/topic/Islam/Tales-and-legends-concerning-religious-figures.

30. Cited in Aksapada, *Analects*, 46.

31. F. Max Müller, trans., *Dhammapada, a Collection of Verses; Being One of the Canonical Books of the Buddhists* (Project Gutenberg, 1999), Dhammapada 209, https://www.gutenberg.org/ebooks/2017.

32. McDonald, *Tao Te Ching*, chap. 56.

33. Cited in Aryeh Kaplan, *Meditation and the Bible* (York Beach, ME: S. Weiser, 1988), 15.

34. Cited in William C. Spohn, *Go and Do Likewise: Jesus and Ethics* (New York: Continuum, 1999), 137.

35. McGill Office of Religious and Spiritual Life, *The MORSL Guide to Faith-Based Meditation* (Montreal: McGill University, 2020), 12, https://www.mcgill.ca/morsl/files/morsl/morsl_meditation_guide_may_5_2020.pdf.

36. Khalsa, "Sri Guru Granth Sahib," 782.

37. Müller, *Dhammapada*, Dhammapada 413.

38. McDonald, *Tao Te Ching*, chap. 16.

39. Black Elk, *The Sacred Pipe*, 115.

40. St. Augustine of Hippo, "Book I: Early Years," in *Confessions*, trans. Henry Chadwick (New York: Oxford University Press, 2008), 3.

41. M. H. Shakir, trans., "Koran 13.28," in *Three Translations of the Koran (Al-Qur'an) Side by Side*, trans. Abdullah Yusuf Ali, Marmaduke William Pickthall, and M. H. Shakir (Project Gutenberg, 2005), https://www.gutenberg.org/ebooks/16955.

42. Shakir, "Koran 59.23," in Ali, Pickthall, and Shakir, *Three Translations*.

43. Khalsa, "Sri Guru Granth Sahib," 32.

44. Khalsa, "Sri Guru Granth Sahib," 11.

CHAPTER 12

1. F. Max Müller, trans., *Dhammapada, a Collection of Verses; Being One of the Canonical Books of the Buddhists* (Project Gutenberg, 1999), Dhammapada 89, https://www.gutenberg.org/ebooks/2017.

2. Müller, *Dhammapada*, Dhammapada 146.

3. M. H. Shakir, trans., "Koran 6.1," in *Three Translations of the Koran*, trans. Abdullah Yusuf Ali, Marmaduke William Pickthall, and M. H. Shakir (Project Gutenberg, 2005), https://www.gutenberg.org/ebooks/16955.

4. Shakir, "Koran 5.16," in Ali, Pickthall, and Shakir, *Three Translations*.

5. Sant Singh Khalsa, trans., "Sri Guru Granth Sahib English Translation," 124, accessed February 29, 2024, http://sikhs.org/english/eg_index.htm.

6. Müller, *Dhammapada*, Dhammapada 224.

7. Müller, *Dhammapada*, Dhammapada 400.

8. Müller, *Dhammapada*, Dhammapada 134.

9. Cited in John Girard and JoAnn Girard, comps., *Sage Sayings: Inspiring Native American Passages for Leaders* (CreateSpace Independent Publishing Platform, 2014), 65. This translation of the Omaha proverb may have been based on the following paper: Alice C. Fletcher and Francis La Flesche, "The Omaha Tribe," in *27th Annual Report of the Bureau of American Ethnology to the Secretary of the Smithsonian Institute, 1905–1906,* by the Bureau of American Ethnology (Washington, DC: US Government Printing Office, 1911), 609.

10. Cited in Girard and Girard, *Sage Sayings*, 67.

11. Shakir, "Koran 3.134," in Ali, Pickthall, and Shakir, *Three Translations*.

12. Abu Amina Elias, "Hadith on Anger: If You Are Angry, Sit or Lie Down," *Daily Hadith Online*, April 3, 2012, https://www.abuaminaelias.com/dailyhadithonline/2012/04/03/angry-stand-sit-lie-down/.

13. Khalsa, "Sri Guru Granth Sahib," 219.

14. Müller, *Dhammapada*, Dhammapada 205.

15. J. H. McDonald, trans., *Tao Te Ching*, chap. 35, updated December 6, 2007, http://www.wright-house.com/religions/taoism/tao-te-ching.html. Note: This translation of the Tao Te Ching uses feminine pronouns; other translations use masculine pronouns. In either case, the teachings of this text are thought to apply to all people regardless of gender.

16. Shakir, "Koran 2.112," in Ali, Pickthall, and Shakir, *Three Translations*.

17. Khalsa, "Sri Guru Granth Sahib," 11.

18. Cited in Michael Garrett and J. T. Garrett, *Native American Faith in America*, ed. J. Gordon Melton (New York: Facts on File, 2003), 98. Also cited (with different punctuation) in Girard and Girard, *Sage Sayings*, 33.

19. Müller, *Dhammapada*, Dhammapada 129 and 130.

20. McDonald, *Tao Te Ching*, chap. 30.

21. McDonald, *Tao Te Ching*, chap. 30.

22. McDonald, *Tao Te Ching*, chap. 68.

23. Cornplanter, Address to the Council, in *Minutes of the Supreme Executive Council of Pennsylvania, From Its Organization to the Termination of the Revolution, Vol. XVI: Containing the Proceedings of the Supreme Executive Council from February 7th, 1789, to December 20th, 1790, Both Days Inclusive,* by the Supreme Executive Council of Pennsylvania (Harrisburg: Theo. Fenn & Co., 1853), 505. Quote also cited (with slight variations) in Girard and JoAnn Girard, *Sage Sayings,* 5.

24. Shakir, "Koran 2.190," in Ali, Pickthall, and Shakir, *Three Translations.*

25. Mustafa Khattab, *The Clear Quran Series: A Thematic English Translation,* ed. Abu-Isa Webb, Aaron Wannamaker, and Hisham Sharif (Lombard, IL: Book of Signs Foundation, 2016), 16.

26. Khalsa, "Sri Guru Granth Sahib," 74.

27. Donald S. Lopez, "Buddhism: Eightfold Path," Encyclopedia Britannica, accessed February 22, 2024, https://www.britannica.com/topic/Eightfold-Path.

28. McDonald, *Tao Te Ching,* chap. 77.

29. Derek Lin, trans., *Tao Te Ching: Annotated and Explained,* foreword by Lama Surya Das (Woodstock, VT: SkyLight Paths, 2015), 154.

30. McDonald, *Tao Te Ching,* chap. 42.

31. Cited in Girard and Girard, *Sage Sayings,* 34.

32. Shakir, "Koran 2.143," in Ali, Pickthall, and Shakir, *Three Translations.*

33. Khattab, *Clear Quran,* 12.

34. Khalsa, "Sri Guru Granth Sahib," 36.

35. Khalsa, "Sri Guru Granth Sahib," 19.

36. Mohinder Singh, "Sikhism: Transcendental and Interfaith Message," in *World Religions: Diversity, Not Dissension,* ed. Anindita N. Balslev (New Delhi: SAGE India, 2014), 37.

CHAPTER 13

1. William Penn, "Prayer," in Michale Smathers, *Let Them Be Not Forgotten: Eulogies Written in a Country Churchyard, 1974–2015* (N.p.: Xlibris, 2016), 383; also found in Bede Jarrett's book of prayers. Rossiter W. Raymond included several lines from Penn's prayer in a poem titled "Death Is Only an Horizon." Carly Simon included a few of these lines in her song "Life Is Eternal."

2. Lawrence Kasdan and George Lucas, screenplay of *Star Wars: Episode VI—Return of the Jedi,* in Star Wars: *The Annotated Screenplays,* annotated by Laurent Bouzereau (New York: Ballantine Books, 1997), 266.

3. F. Max Müller, trans., *Dhammapada, a Collection of Verses; Being One of the Canonical Books of the Buddhists* (Project Gutenberg, 1999), Dhammapada 151, https://www.gutenberg.org/ebooks/2017.

4. Bernard Down, "Death in Classical Daoist Thought," Philosophy Now, accessed February 22, 2024, https://philosophynow.org/issues/27/Death_in_Classical_Daoist_Thought.

5. George Lucas, dir., *Star Wars: Episode III—Revenge of the Sith*, written by George Lucas (San Francisco: Lucasfilm, 2019), DVD, 0:33:27–0:34:41.

6. Cited in John Girard and JoAnn Girard, comps., *Sage Sayings: Inspiring Native American Passages for Leaders* (CreateSpace Independent Publishing Platform, 2014), 29.

7. Cited in Michael Garrett and J. T. Garrett, *Native American Faith in America*, ed. J. Gordon Melton (New York: Facts on File, 2003), 98. Also cited (with different punctuation) in Girard and Girard, *Sage Sayings*, 33.

8. Cited in Garrett and Garrett, *Native American Faith*, 98. Also cited in Girard and Girard, *Sage Sayings*, 14.

9. M. H. Shakir, trans., "Koran 3.185," in *Three Translations of the Koran (Al-Qur'an) Side by Side*, trans. Abdullah Yusuf Ali, Marmaduke William Pickthall, and M. H. Shakir (Project Gutenberg, 2005), https://www.gutenberg.org/ebooks/16955.

10. Shakir, "Koran 16.61," in Ali, Pickthall, and Shakir, *Three Translations*.

11. Sant Singh Khalsa, trans., "Sri Guru Granth Sahib English Translation," 15, accessed February 29, 2024, http://sikhs.org/english/eg_index.htm.

12. Kasdan and Lucas, screenplay of *Return of the Jedi*, 266.

13. Down, "Death in Classical Daoist Thought."

14. "Daoism: Xian," Encyclopedia Britannica, accessed February 22, 2024, https://www.britannica.com/topic/xian-Daoism.

15. "Death and the Afterlife," BBC, accessed February 22, 2024, https://www.bbc.co.uk/bitesize/guides/zcbgh39/revision/3.

16. Shakir, "Koran 18.107," in Ali, Pickthall, and Shakir, *Three Translations*.

17. Shakir, "Koran 2.25," in Ali, Pickthall, and Shakir, *Three Translations*.

18. Shakir, "Koran 25.15," in Ali, Pickthall, and Shakir, *Three Translations*.

19. Cited in Aksapada, comp., *The Analects of Rumi* (N.p.: n.p., n.d.), 25.

20. Cited in Aksapada, *Analects*, 114.

21. Khalsa, "Sri Guru Granth Sahib," 850.

22. Christine Leigh Heyrman, "Native American Religion in Early America," TeacherServe, revised 2008, https://nationalhumanitiescenter.org/tserve/eighteen/ekeyinfo/natrel.htm.

23. George Lucas, screenplay of *Star Wars: Episode IV—A New Hope*, in Bouzereau, *Annotated Screenplays*, 59.

24. Müller, *Dhammapada*, Dhammapada 23.

25. "15.2 World Religions," OpenStax, accessed February 22, 2024, https://openstax.org/books/introduction-sociology-2e/pages/15-2-world-religions.

26. Eman M. Elshaikh, "Read: Daoism," Khan Academy, accessed February 22, 2024, https://www.khanacademy.org/humanities/whp-origins/era-3-cities-societies-and-empires-6000-bce-to-700-c-e/35-development-of-belief-systems-betaa/a/read-daoism-beta.

27. J. H. McDonald, trans., *Tao Te Ching*, chap. 16, updated December 6, 2007, http://www.wright-house.com/religions/taoism/tao-te-ching.html.

28. McDonald, *Tao Te Ching*, chap. 29.

29. Mourning Dove, *Mourning Dove: A Salishan Autobiography*, ed. Jay Miller (Lincoln: University of Nebraska Press, 1990), 69. Also cited (with different punctuation) in Girard and Girard, *Sage Sayings*, 25.

30. Kamil Mufti, "Meaning of Life in Islam," *Arab News*, updated January 22, 2016, https://www.arabnews.com/islam-perspective/news/868496.

31. Shakir, "Koran 3.191," in Ali, Pickthall, and Shakir, *Three Translations*.

32. See Mohsin Khan's translation at "Verse (3:191)—English Translation," Quranic Arabic Corpus, accessed February 22, 2024, https://corpus.quran.com/translation.jsp?chapter=3&verse=191.

33. Khalsa, "Sri Guru Granth Sahib," 744.

34. Lucas, screenplay of *A New Hope*, 59.

CHAPTER 14

1. Cited in Aksapada, comp., *1400 Lessons from the 14th Dalai Lama* (N.p.: n.p., n.d.), 48.

2. Melissa de la Cruz, *Lost in Time* (New York: Hyperion, 2011), 237.

3. Veronica Roth, *Divergent* (London: HarperCollins, 2012), 476.

4. George Lucas, dir., *Star Wars: Episode III—Revenge of the Sith*, written by George Lucas (Lucasfilm, 2019), DVD, 0:45:43–0:46:00.

5. F. Max Müller, trans., *Dhammapada, a Collection of Verses; Being One of the Canonical Books of the Buddhists* (Project Gutenberg, 1999), Dhammapada 177, https://www.gutenberg.org/ebooks/2017.

6. Müller, *Dhammapada*, Dhammapada 223.

7. J. H. McDonald, trans., *Tao Te Ching*, chap. 7, updated December 6, 2007, http://www.wright-house.com/religions/taoism/tao-te-ching.html.

8. McDonald, *Tao Te Ching*, chap. 7.

9. Derek Lin, trans., *Tao Te Ching: Annotated and Explained*, foreword by Lama Surya Das (Woodstock, VT: SkyLight Paths, 2015), 14.

10. Cited in John Girard and JoAnn Girard, comps., *Sage Sayings: Inspiring Native American Passages for Leaders* (CreateSpace Independent Publishing Platform, 2014), 17.

11. Cited in Guy Zona, comp., *The Soul Would Have No Rainbow If the Eyes Had No Tears—and Other Native American Proverbs* (New York: Touchstone, 1994), 13. Also cited in Girard and Girard, *Sage Sayings*, 19.

12. Charles Alexander Eastman, *The Soul of an Indian and Other Writings from Ohiyesa (Charles Alexander Eastman)*, ed. Kent Nerburn (Novato, CA: New World Library, 2001), 28. Also cited (with slight variations) in Girard and Girard, *Sage Sayings*, 21.

13. M. H. Shakir, trans., "Koran 59.9," in *Three Translations of the Koran (Al-Qur'an) Side by Side*, trans. Abdullah Yusuf Ali, Marmaduke William Pickthall, and M. H. Shakir (Project Gutenberg, 2005), https://www.gutenberg.org/ebooks/16955.

14. Sant Singh Khalsa, trans., "Sri Guru Granth Sahib English Translation," 125, accessed February 29, 2024, http://sikhs.org/english/eg_index.htm.

15. Leigh Brackett and Lawrence Kasdan, screenplay of *Star Wars: Episode V—The Empire Strikes Back* in Star Wars: *The Annotated Screenplays*, annotated by Laurent Bouzereau (New York: Ballantine Books, 1997), 180.

16. Müller, *Dhammapada*, Dhammapada 121 and 122.

17. McDonald, *Tao Te Ching*, chap. 79.

18. Cited Girard and Girard, *Sage Sayings*, 5.

19. Cited in Girard and Girard, *Sage Sayings*, 15. See also Emory Sekaquaptewa, Kenneth C. Hill, and Dorothy K. Washburn, *Hopi Katsina Songs* (Lincoln: University of Nebraska Press, 2015), 358.

20. Shakir, "Koran 5.93," in Ali, Pickthall, and Shakir, *Three Translations*.

21. Shakir, "Koran 98.7," in Ali, Pickthall, and Shakir, *Three Translations*.

22. Khalsa, "Sri Guru Granth Sahib," 84.

23. Khalsa, "Sri Guru Granth Sahib," 16.

24. Brackett and Kasdan, screenplay of *The Empire Strikes Back*, 180.

25. "Newton's Third Law," Physics Classroom, accessed February 22, 2024, https://www.physicsclassroom.com/class/newtlaws/Lesson-4/Newton-s-Third-Law.

26. Müller, *Dhammapada*, Dhammapada 66.

27. Müller, *Dhammapada*, Dhammapada 71.

28. Shakir, "Koran 4.79," in Ali, Pickthall, and Shakir, *Three Translations*.

29. Mustafa Khattab, *The Clear Quran Series: A Thematic English Translation*, ed. Abu-Isa Webb, Aaron Wannamaker, and Hisham Sharif (Lombard, IL: Book of Signs Foundation, 2016), 48–50.

30. Khalsa, "Sri Guru Granth Sahib," 78.

31. Khalsa, "Sri Guru Granth Sahib," 135.

CHAPTER 15

1. Albert Einstein, "What Life Means to Einstein," interview by George S. Viereck, *Saturday Evening Post*, October 26, 1929. Reprinted in *Glimpses of the Great*, by George S. Viereck (New York: Macauley, 1930), 446. Quote cited in Alice Calaprice, ed., *The Ultimate Quotable Einstein*, foreword by Freeman Dyson (Princeton, NJ: Princeton University Press, 2019), 435.

2. Dean Koontz, *The Darkest Evening of the Year* (New York: Random House, 2007), 442.

3. Cited in Tian Dayton, *One Foot in Front of the Other: Daily Affirmations for Recovery* (Deerfield Beach, FL: Health Communications, 2013), 329.

4. George Lucas, screenplay of *Star Wars: Episode IV—A New Hope*, in Star Wars: *The Annotated Screenplays*, annotated by Laurent Bouzereau (New York: Ballantine Books, 1997), 61.

5. Leigh Brackett and Lawrence Kasdan, screenplay of *Star Wars: Episode V—The Empire Strikes Back*, in Bouzereau, *Annotated Screenplays*, 216.

6. Thomas Egenes, trans., "Yoga Sutra 3.33," in *Maharishi Patañjali Yoga Sūtra* (Fairfield, IA: 1st World Publishing, 2010), 92.

7. Akihisa Kondo, "Intuition in Zen Buddhism," *American Journal of Psychoanalysis* 12, no. 1 (1952): 10.

8. Ted Kardash, "Taoism—Ancient Wisdom for a Modern World: The Tao of Daily Living," Pacific College of Health and Science, March 25, 2015, https://www.pacificcollege.edu/news/blog/2015/03/25/taoism---ancient-wisdom-for-a-modern-world-the-tao-of-daily-living.

9. J. H. McDonald, trans., *Tao Te Ching*, chap. 52, updated December 6, 2007, http://www.wright-house.com/religions/taoism/tao-te-ching.html.

10. Cited in John Girard and JoAnn Girard, comps., *Sage Sayings: Inspiring Native American Passages for Leaders* (CreateSpace Independent Publishing Platform, 2014), 34.

11. *New Oxford American Dictionary*, 3rd ed. (New York: Oxford University Press, 2010).

12. "Sufism: Kashf," Encyclopedia Britannica, accessed February 22, 2024, https://www.britannica.com/topic/kashf.

13. Cited in Encyclopedia Britannica, "Sufism: Kashf."

14. Sant Singh Khalsa, trans., "Sri Guru Granth Sahib English Translation," 893, accessed February 29, 2024, http://sikhs.org/english/eg_index.htm.

15. Khalsa, "Sri Guru Granth Sahib," 927.

16. F. Max Müller, trans., *Dhammapada, a Collection of Verses; Being One of the Canonical Books of the Buddhists* (Project Gutenberg, 1999), Dhammapada 89, https://www.gutenberg.org/ebooks/2017.

17. Müller, *Dhammapada*, Dhammapada 401.

18. Müller, *Dhammapada*, Dhammapada 414.

19. Khalsa, "Sri Guru Granth Sahib," 61.

20. McDonald, *Tao Te Ching*, chaps. 2, 53, 44, and 46.

21. *New Oxford American Dictionary*.

22. M. H. Shakir, trans, "Koran 104.1–3," in *Three Translations of the Koran (Al-Qur'an) Side by Side*, trans. Abdullah Yusuf Ali, Marmaduke William Pickthall, and M. H. Shakir (Project Gutenberg, 2005), https://www.gutenberg.org/ebooks/16955.

23. Khalsa, "Sri Guru Granth Sahib," 155.

24. Khalsa, "Sri Guru Granth Sahib," 250.

25. Vernon Katz and Thomas Egenes, trans., "Katha Upanishad 1.2.6," in *The Upanishads: A New Translation* (New York: Jeremy P. Tarcher/Penguin, 2015), 51.

26. *New Oxford American Dictionary*.

27. Müller, *Dhammapada*, Dhammapada 199, 216, and 248.

28. Red Cloud, "I Represent the Whole Sioux Nation, and They Will Be Bound by What I Say" (1870), in *Indian Oratory: Famous Speeches by Noted Indian Chieftains,*

comp. W. C. Vanderwerth, foreword by William R. Carmack (Norman: University of Oklahoma Press, 1971), 189. Quote also cited (with different punctuation) in Girard and Girard, *Sage Sayings*, 24.

29. George Lucas, screenplay of *Star Wars: Episode IV—A New Hope*, in Bouzereau, *Annotated Screenplays*, 59.

30. Lawrence Kasdan and George Lucas, screenplay of *Star Wars: Episode VI—Return of the Jedi*, in Bouzereau, *Annotated Screenplays*, 292.

31. Müller, *Dhammapada*, Dhammapada 223.

32. McDonald, *Tao Te Ching*, chap. 29.

33. Shakir, "Koran 59.9," in Ali, Pickthall, and Shakir, *Three Translations*.

34. Khalsa, "Sri Guru Granth Sahib," 125.

35. Khalsa, "Sri Guru Granth Sahib," 126.

36. Cited in Girard and Girard, *Sage Sayings*, 27.

37. Shakir, "Koran 3.144," in Ali, Pickthall, and Shakir, *Three Translations*.

38. Shakir, "Koran 14.7," in Ali, Pickthall, and Shakir, *Three Translations*.

39. Khalsa, "Sri Guru Granth Sahib," 73.

40. Müller, *Dhammapada*, Dhammapada 414; emphasis added.

41. McDonald, *Tao Te Ching*, chap. 46.

CHAPTER 16

1. F. Max Müller, trans., *Dhammapada, a Collection of Verses; Being One of the Canonical Books of the Buddhists* (Project Gutenberg, 1999), Dhammapada 81, https://www.gutenberg.org/ebooks/2017.

2. Müller, *Dhammapada*, Dhammapada 81 and 82.

3. J. H. McDonald, trans., *Tao Te Ching* chap. 33, updated December 6, 2007, http://www.wright-house.com/religions/taoism/tao-te-ching.html.

4. Charles Alexander Eastman, "The Indian and the Moral Code," in *The Outlook*, reprinted in *Liahona: The Elder's Journal* 8, no. 33 (January 1911): 514. Quote also cited (with slight variations) in John Girard and JoAnn Girard, comps., *Sage Sayings: Inspiring Native American Passages for Leaders* (CreateSpace Independent Publishing Platform, 2014), 17.

5. Cited in Girard and Girard, *Sage Sayings*, 31.

6. M. H. Shakir, trans., "Koran 11.52," in *Three Translations of the Koran (Al-Qur'an) Side by Side*, trans. Abdullah Yusuf Ali, Marmaduke William Pickthall, and M. H. Shakir (Project Gutenberg, 2005), https://www.gutenberg.org/ebooks/16955.

7. Sant Singh Khalsa, trans., "Sri Guru Granth Sahib English Translation," 144, accessed February 29, 2024, https://sikhs.org/english/eg_index.htm.

8. Khalsa, "Sri Guru Granth Sahib," 51.

9. Khalsa, "Sri Guru Granth Sahib," 51.

10. Christopher Titmuss, "Four Truths of the Noble Ones," accessed February 22, 2024, https://www.christophertitmuss.net/four-truths-of-the-noble-ones; "Basics

of Buddhism," PBS, accessed February 22, 2024, https://www.pbs.org/edens/thailand/buddhism.htm.

11. "Four Truths of the Noble Ones," Samye Institute, accessed February 22, 2024, https://www.samyeinstitute.org/wiki/four-truths-of-the-noble-ones/; "The Noble Eightfold Path," Pranic Healers, accessed February 22, 2024, https://www.thepranichealers.com/eightfold-path.

12. McDonald, *Tao Te Ching*, chap. 21.

13. Cited in Girard and Girard, *Sage Sayings*, 34; emphasis added.

14. Shakir, "Koran 10.5," in Ali, Pickthall, and Shakir, *Three Translations*; emphasis added.

15. Khalsa, "Sri Guru Granth Sahib," 124.

CHAPTER 17

1. Leigh Brackett and Lawrence Kasdan, screenplay of *Star Wars: Episode V—The Empire Strikes Back*, in Star Wars*: The Annotated Screenplays*, annotated by Laurent Bouzereau (New York: Ballantine Books, 1997), 187.

2. This quote is often attributed to Pierre Teilhard de Chardin; however, evidence suggests that it was actually written by Wayne W. Dyer. See "You Are Not a Human Being Having a Spiritual Experience. You Are a Spiritual Being Having a Human Experience," Quote Investigator, June 20, 2019, https://quoteinvestigator.com/2019/06/20/spiritual/.

3. D. Y. F. Ho, "Selfhood and Identity in Confucianism, Taoism, Buddhism, and Hinduism: Contrasts with the West," *Journal for the Theory of Social Behaviour* 25, no. 2 (1995): 115–39.

4. Bernard Down, "Death in Classical Daoist Thought," Philosophy Now, accessed February 22, 2024, https://philosophynow.org/issues/27/Death_in_Classical_Daoist_Thought.

5. Down, "Death in Classical Daoist Thought."

6. Jalal al-Din Rumi, "We Can See the Truth in Your Eyes," in *Rumi: In the Arms of the Beloved*, trans. Jonathan Star (New York: Penguin, 2008), 3.

7. Sant Singh Khalsa, trans., "Sri Guru Granth Sahib English Translation," 96, accessed February 29, 2024, https://sikhs.org/english/eg_index.htm.

8. F. Max Müller, trans., *Dhammapada, a Collection of Verses; Being One of the Canonical Books of the Buddhists* (Project Gutenberg, 1999), Dhammapada 205, https://www.gutenberg.org/ebooks/2017.

9. Cited in Livia Kohn, ed., *The Taoist Experience: An Anthology* (Albany: State University of New York Press, 1993), 98.

10. M. H. Shakir, trans., "Koran 7.153," in *Three Translations of The Koran (Al-Qur'an) Side by Side*, trans. Abdullah Yusuf Ali, Marmaduke William Pickthall, and M. H. Shakir (Project Gutenberg, 2005), https://www.gutenberg.org/ebooks/16955.

11. Khalsa, "Sri Guru Granth Sahib," 93 and 88.

CHAPTER 18

1. Thomas Egenes, introduction to *The Upanishads: A New Translation*, trans. Vernon Katz and Thomas Egenes (New York: Jeremy P. Tarcher/Penguin, 2015), 3.

2. George Lucas, screenplay of *Star Wars: Episode IV—A New Hope*, in Star Wars*: The Annotated Screenplays*, annotated by Laurent Bouzereau (New York: Ballantine Books, 1997), 59.

3. Leigh Brackett and Lawrence Kasdan, screenplay of *Star Wars: Episode V—The Empire Strikes Back*, in Bouzereau, *Annotated Screenplays*, 187.

4. "'You've Got to Find What You Love,' Jobs Says," *Stanford News*, June 12, 2005, https://news.stanford.edu/2005/06/12/youve-got-find-love-jobs-says/.

5. Lucas, screenplay of *A New Hope*, 59.

6. Cited in Ryder Windham, Star Wars Episode I: The Phantom Menace *Movie Scrapbook* (New York: Random House, 1999), 13.

7. Brackett and Kasdan, screenplay of *The Empire Strikes Back*, 187.

8. Egenes, introduction, 3.

9. Vernon Katz and Thomas Egenes, trans., "Mundaka Upanishad 3.1.6," in *The Upanishads: A New Translation* (New York: Jeremy P. Tarcher/Penguin, 2015), 98.

10. Nanak was the first Sikh guru and the founder of Sikhism. Sant Singh Khalsa, trans., "Sri Guru Granth Sahib English Translation," 953, accessed February 29, 2024, http://sikhs.org/english/eg_index.htm.

11. Cited in Aksapada, comp., *1400 Lessons from the 14th Dalai Lama* (N.p.: n.p., n.d.), 27.

12. "Spirit of truth" means the Holy Spirit within every Christian.

13. M. H. Shakir, trans., "Koran 17.81," in *Three Translations of The Koran (Al-Qur'an) Side by Side*, trans. Abdullah Yusuf Ali, Marmaduke William Pickthall, and M. H. Shakir (Project Gutenberg, 2005), https://www.gutenberg.org/ebooks/16955.

APPENDIX A

1. Frederick Travis and Jonathan Shear, "Focused Attention, Open Monitoring and Automatic Self-Transcending: Categories to Organize Meditations from Vedic, Buddhist and Chinese Traditions," *Consciousness and Cognition* 19, no. 4 (February 2010): 1112.

2. Travis and Shear, "Categories to Organize Meditations," 1114.

3. Travis and Shear, "Categories to Organize Meditations," 1115.

BIBLIOGRAPHY

Abrams, J. J., dir. *Star Wars: Episode VII—The Force Awakens.* Written by Lawrence Kasdan, J. J. Abrams, and Michael Arndt. Based on characters by George Lucas. 2015; San Francisco: Lucasfilm and Bad Robot Productions, 2019. DVD.

———. *Star Wars: Episode IX—The Rise of Skywalker.* Screenplay by Chris Terrio and J. J. Abrams. Story by Derek Connolly, Colin Trevorrow, J. J. Abrams, and Chris Terrio. Based on characters by George Lucas. 2019; San Francisco: Lucasfilm and Bad Robot Productions, 2020. DVD.

Adherents. "Religious Affiliation of Director George Lucas." May 27, 2005. https://web.archive.org/web/20050612235541/http:/www.adherents.com/people/pl/George_Lucas.html.

Aiyar, K. Narayanaswami, trans. *Thirty Minor Upaniṣads.* Edited by Madhu Khanna. New Delhi: Tantra Foundation, 2011. https://www.wisdomlib.org/hinduism/book/thirty-minor-upanishads/d/doc217031.html.

Aksapada, comp. *1400 Lessons from the 14th Dalai Lama.* N.p.: n.p., n.d.

———. *The Analects of Rumi.* N.p.: n.p., n.d.

Aleksander, Irina. "Look Who's Meditating Now." *New York Times*, March 18, 2011. https://www.nytimes.com/2011/03/20/fashion/20TM.html.

Ali, Abdullah Yusuf, Marmaduke William Pickthall, and M. H. Shakir, trans. *Three Translations of the Koran (Al-Qur'an) Side by Side.* Project Gutenberg, 2005. https://www.gutenberg.org/ebooks/16955.

Allers, Roger, and Rob Minkoff, dirs. *The Lion King.* Screenplay by Irene Mecchi, Jonathan Roberts, and Linda Woolverton. Burbank, CA: Walt Disney Pictures and Walt Disney Feature Animation, 1994.

American Film Institute. "100 Greatest Movie Quotes of All Time." Accessed February 22, 2024. https://www.afi.com/afis-100-years-100-movie-quotes/.

Andrew, Scott. *The Rugged Entrepreneur: What Every Disruptive Business Leader Should Know.* New York: Forefront Books, 2021.

Armstrong, Karen. "Towards Interfaith Understanding." In *Faith, Identity, Cohesion: Building a Better Future*, edited by Jolene Jerard and Amanda Huan, 33–41. Singapore: World Scientific Publishing, 2020.

Augustine of Hippo, Saint. "Book I: Early Years." In *Confessions*, translated by Henry Chadwick, 3–23. New York: Oxford University Press, 2008.

BarbaRossa. "We Are All Connected—Neil deGrasse Tyson." YouTube, November 12, 2010. Video. https://www.youtube.com/watch?v=CtWB90bVUO8.

Bawa Muhaiyaddeen, M. R. *To Die Before Death: The Sufi Way of Life*. Philadelphia: Fellowship Press, 1997.

BBC. "Death and the Afterlife." Accessed February 22, 2024. https://www.bbc.co .uk/bitesize/guides/zcbgh39/revision/3.

———. "Theravada Buddhism." Updated October 2, 2002. https://www.bbc.co.uk /religion/religions/buddhism/subdivisions/theravada_1.shtml.

Bedagi (Big Thunder). "Hunting the Moose." In *The Indians' Book: An Offering by the American Indians of Indian Lore, Musical and Narrative, to Form a Record of the Songs and Legends of Their Race*. Recorded and edited by Natalie Curtis. New York: Harper and Brothers, 1907.

Black Elk. *The Sacred Pipe: Black Elk's Account of the Seven Rites of the Oglala Sioux*. Recorded and edited by Joseph Epes Brown. Oklahoma: University of Oklahoma Press, 2012.

Bloomfield, Maurice. *The Religion of the Veda: The Ancient Religion of India (From Rig-Veda to Upanishads)*. New York: G. P. Putnam's Sons, 1908.

Boundless. "The Rise of Hinduism." In *Boundless World History*. Edited by Lumen Learning. New York: State University of New York OER Services, 2018. https: //courses.lumenlearning.com/suny-hccc-worldcivilization/chapter/the-rise-of -hinduism/.

Brackett, Leigh, and Lawrence Kasdan. Screenplay of *Star Wars: Episode V—The Empire Strikes Back*. Based on a story by George Lucas. In *Star Wars: The Annotated Screenplays*, annotated by Laurent Bouzereau, 121–27. New York: Ballantine Books, 1997.

Calaprice, Alice, ed. *The Ultimate Quotable Einstein*. Foreword by Freeman Dyson. Princeton, NJ: Princeton University Press, 2019.

Chang, Larry, ed. *Wisdom for the Soul: Five Millennia of Prescriptions for Spiritual Healing*. Washington, DC: Gnosophia, 2006.

Cine Extras. "Deleted Scenes—Yoda Communes with Qui-Gon—*Star Wars Episode III Revenge of the Sith* 2005." YouTube, May 12, 2020. Video. https://www.youtube .com/watch?v=BnMWRkCkEks.

Cornplanter. "Address to the Council." In Supreme Executive Council of Pennsylvania, *Minutes of the Supreme Executive Council of Pennsylvania, From Its Organization to the Termination of the Revolution, Vol. XVI: Containing the Proceedings of the Supreme Executive Council from February 7th, 1789, to December 20th, 1790, Both Days Inclusive*, 501–6. Harrisburg: Theo. Fenn & Co., 1853.

Dayton, Tian. *One Foot in Front of the Other: Daily Affirmations for Recovery*. Deerfield Beach, FL: Health Communications, 2013.

de la Cruz, Melissa. *Lost in Time*. New York: Hyperion, 2011.

Down, Bernard. "Death in Classical Daoist Thought." Philosophy Now. Accessed February 22, 2024. https://philosophynow.org/issues/27/Death_in_Classical _Daoist_Thought.

Eastman, Charles Alexander. "The Indian and the Moral Code." In *The Outlook*. Reprinted in *Liahona: The Elder's Journal* 8, no. 33 (January 1911): 514–19.

———. *The Soul of an Indian and Other Writings from Ohiyesa (Charles Alexander Eastman)*. Edited by Kent Nerburn. Novato, CA: New World Library, 2001.

Edutopia. "How Daily Meditation Improves Behavior." February 23, 2012. https:// www.edutopia.org/stw-student-stress-meditation-overview-video.

Egenes, Thomas. Introduction to *The Upanishads: A New Translation*, translated by Vernon Katz and Thomas Egenes, 1–28. New York: Jeremy P. Tarcher/Penguin, 2015.

———, trans. *Maharishi Patañjali Yoga Sūtra*. Fairfield, IA: 1st World Publishing, 2010.

Einstein, Albert. "What Life Means to Einstein." Interview by George S. Viereck. *Saturday Evening Post*, October 26, 1929. Reprinted in George S. Viereck, *Glimpses of the Great*. New York: Macauley, 1930.

Elias, Abu Amina. "Hadith on Anger: If You Are Angry, Sit or Lie Down." *Daily Hadith Online*, April 3, 2012. https://www.abuaminaelias.com/dailyhadithonline /2012/04/03/angry-stand-sit-lie-down.

Elshaikh, Eman M. "Read: Daoism." Khan Academy. Accessed February 22, 2024. https://www.khanacademy.org/humanities/whp-origins/era-3-cities -societies-and-empires-6000-bce-to-700-c-e/35-development-of-belief-systems -betaa/a/read-daoism-beta.

Encyclopedia Britannica. "Daoism: Xian." Accessed February 22, 2024. https:// www.britannica.com/topic/xian-Daoism.

———. "Sufism: Kashf." Accessed February 22, 2024. https://www.britannica.com /topic/kashf.

"Filmmaker Introduces Veterans to Meditation." *Wall Street Journal*, updated November 26, 2010. https://www.wsj.com/articles/SB10001424052748704638 304575636911988306800.

Fitzgerald, Michael Oren, and Judith Fitzgerald, eds. *Indian Spirit*. Bloomington, IN: World Wisdom, 2006.

Fletcher, Alice C., and Francis La Flesche. "The Omaha Tribe." In Bureau of American Ethnology, *27th Annual Report of the Bureau of American Ethnology to the Secretary of the Smithsonian Institute, 1905–1906*, 15–654. Washington, DC: US Government Printing Office, 1911.

Gandhi, Mahatma. "Mahatma Gandhi's Address to Missionaries." *Missionary Review of the World* 49, no. 1 (January 1926): 34–38.

Garrett, Michael, and J. T. Garrett. *Native American Faith in America*. Edited by J. Gordon Melton. New York: Facts on File, 2003.

Girard, John, and JoAnn Girard, comps. *Sage Sayings: Inspiring Native American Passages for Leaders*. CreateSpace Independent Publishing Platform, 2014.

Golembiewski, Kate. "Life after Death? Cryonicists Try to Defy Mortality by Freezing Bodies." *Discover Magazine*, October 14, 2022. https://www.discovermagazine.com/technology/will-cryonically-frozen-bodies-ever-be-brought-back-to-life.

Heyrman, Christine Leigh. "Native American Religion in Early America." TeacherServe, revised 2008. https://nationalhumanitiescenter.org/tserve/eighteen/ekeyinfo/natrel.htm.

Hijiya, James A. "The *Gita* of J. Robert Oppenheimer." *Proceedings of the American Philosophical Society* 144, no. 2 (June 2000): 123–67.

"Hollywood's 100 Favorite Movie Quotes." *Hollywood Reporter*, February 24, 2016. https://www.hollywoodreporter.com/lists/best-movie-quotes-hollywoods-top-867142/.

Ho, D. Y. F. "Selfhood and Identity in Confucianism, Taoism, Buddhism, and Hinduism: Contrasts with the West." *Journal for the Theory of Social Behaviour* 25, no. 2 (1995): 115–39.

Johnson, Rian, dir. *Star Wars: Episode VIII—The Last Jedi*. Written by Rian Johnson. Based on characters by George Lucas. 2017; San Francisco: Lucasfilm, 2019. DVD.

Kaminski, Michael. *The Secret History of* Star Wars: *The Art of Storytelling and the Making of a Modern Epic*. Ontario: Legacy Books Press, 2008.

Kaplan, Aryeh. *Meditation and the Bible*. York Beach, ME: S. Weiser, 1988.

Kardash, Ted. "Taoism—Ancient Wisdom for a Modern World: The Tao of Daily Living." Pacific College of Health and Science, March 25, 2015. https://www.pacificcollege.edu/news/blog/2015/03/25/taoism---ancient-wisdom-for-a-modern-world-the-tao-of-daily-living.

Kasdan, Lawrence, and George Lucas. Screenplay of *Star Wars: Episode VI—Return of the Jedi*. In Star Wars: *The Annotated Screenplays—A New Hope, The Empire Strikes Back, Return of the Jedi*, annotated by Laurent Bouzereau, 229–20. New York: Ballantine Books, 1997.

Katz, Vernon, and Thomas Egenes, trans. *The Upanishads: A New Translation*. New York: Jeremy P. Tarcher/Penguin, 2015.

Kershner, Irvin, dir. *Star Wars: Episode V—The Empire Strikes Back*. Screenplay by Leigh Brackett and Lawrence Kasdan. Story by George Lucas. 1980; San Francisco: Lucasfilm, 2019. DVD.

Khalsa, Sant Singh, trans. "Sri Guru Granth Sahib English Translation." Accessed February 29, 2024. http://sikhs.org/english/eg_index.htm.

Khan, Inayat. "Saum." In *The Heart of Sufism: Essential Writings of Hazrat Inayat Khan*, edited by H. J. Witteveen, 80–81. Boston: Shambala Publications, 1999.

Khattab, Mustafa. *The Clear Quran Series: A Thematic English Translation*. Edited by Abu-Isa Webb, Aaron Wannamaker, and Hisham Sharif. Lombard, IL: Book of Signs Foundation, 2016.

Kleinschnitz, Kurt Warren. "An Investigation into Field Effects of Consciousness from the Perspectives of Maharishi's Vedic Science and Physics." PhD diss.,

Maharishi International University, 1997. https://www.proquest.com/docview /304404768.

Knockwood, Noel. "The Seven Sacred Prayer." In *Science and the Management of Protected Areas: Proceedings of an International Conference Held at Acadia University, Nova Scotia, Canada, 14–19 May 1991*, edited by J. H. M. Willison, S. Bondrup-Nielsen, C. Drysdale, T. B. Herman, N. W. P. Munro, and T. L. Pollock. Amsterdam: Elsevier Science, 1992.

Kohn, Livia, ed. *The Taoist Experience: An Anthology.* Albany: State University of New York Press, 1993.

Kondo, Akihisa. "Intuition in Zen Buddhism." *American Journal of Psychoanalysis* 12, no. 1 (1952): 10–14.

Koontz, Dean. *The Darkest Evening of the Year.* New York: Random House, 2007.

Kroyer, Bill, dir. *FernGully: The Last Rainforest.* Screenplay by Jim Cox. Original stories by Diana Young. N.p.: FAI Films, Interscope Communications, Kroyer Films, and Youngheart Productions, 1992.

Larsen, Stephen, and Robin Larsen. *Joseph Campbell: A Fire in the Mind—The Authorized Biography.* Rochester, VT: Inner Traditions, 2002.

Liezi. "Book II: The Yellow Emperor." In *Taoist Teachings from the Book of Lieh Tzu*, translated by Lionel Giles, 36–57. New York: E. P. Dutton, 1912.

Lin, Derek, trans. *Tao Te Ching: Annotated and Explained.* Foreword by Lama Surya Das. Woodstock, VT: SkyLight Paths, 2015.

Lokeswarananda, Swami, trans. *Chandogya Upanishad.* Kolkata, India: Ramakrishna Mission Institute of Culture, 2017. Updated March 14, 2019. https://www .wisdomlib.org/hinduism/book/chandogya-upanishad-english.

Lopez, Donald S. "Buddhism: Eightfold Path." Encyclopedia Britannica, updated April 1, 2024. https://www.britannica.com/topic/Eightfold-Path.

Lucas, George. "The Mythology of 'Star Wars' with George Lucas." Interview by Bill Moyers. BillMoyers.com, June 18, 1999. https://billmoyers.com/content/ mythology-of-star-wars-george-lucas/.

———. Screenplay of *Star Wars: Episode IV—A New Hope.* In *Star Wars: The Annotated Screenplays—A New Hope, The Empire Strikes Back, Return of the Jedi*, annotated by Laurent Bouzereau, 1–120. New York: Ballantine Books, 1997.

———, dir. *Star Wars: Episode I—The Phantom Menace.* Written by George Lucas. 1999; San Francisco: Lucasfilm, 2019. DVD.

———, dir. *Star Wars: Episode II—Attack of the Clones.* Screenplay by George Lucas and Jonathan Hales. 2002; San Francisco: Lucasfilm, 2019. DVD.

———, dir. *Star Wars: Episode III—Revenge of the Sith.* Written by George Lucas. 2005; San Francisco: Lucasfilm, 2019. DVD.

———, dir. *Star Wars: Episode IV—A New Hope.* Written by George Lucas. 1977; San Francisco: Lucasfilm, 2019. DVD.

———. "The Star Wars—From the Adventures of Luke Starkiller—Third Draft." Starkiller, March 31, 2010. https://www.starwarz.com/starkiller/the-star-wars -from-the-adventures-of-luke-starkiller-third-draft/.

———. "Star Wars (Public Version of Fourth Draft)." Starkiller, March 31, 2010. https://www.starwarz.com/starkiller/star-wars-public-version-of-fourth-draft/.

Maharishi Mahesh Yogi. *Constitution of India Fulfilled through Maharishi's Transcendental Meditation.* India: Age of Enlightenment Publications, 1999.

———. *Maharishi Mahesh Yogi on the Bhagavad-Gita: A New Translation and Commentary with Sanskrit Text.* Fairfield, IA: Maharishi International University Press, 2015.

———. *Science of Being and Art of Living.* New York: Plume, 2001.

———, trans. "Vedic Expressions Used in Maharishi Vedic Science." Fairfield, IA: Department of Maharishi Vedic Science, Maharishi International University, n.d.

Maharishi Mahesh Yogi and Vernon Katz, trans. *Bhagavad-Gita: All 18 Chapters.* Fairfield, IA: Department of Maharishi Vedic Science, Maharishi International University, n.d. Electronic file.

Marquand, Richard, dir. *Star Wars: Episode VI—Return of the Jedi.* Screenplay by Lawrence Kasdan and George Lucas. Story by George Lucas. 1983; San Francisco: Lucasfilm, 2019. DVD.

Maruyama, Takao. "Buddha's Supernatural Powers in the Lotus Sutra." Paper presented at the 34th International Congress of Asian and North African Studies, Hong Kong, August 1993.

Mason, L. I., C. N. Alexander, F. T. Travis, G. March, D. W. Orme-Johnson, J. Gackenbach, D. C. Mason, M. Rainforth and K. G. Walton. "Electrophysiological Correlates of Higher States of Consciousness During Sleep in Long-Term Practitioners of the Transcendental Meditation Program." *Sleep* 20, no. 2 (February 1997): 102–10. https://pubmed.ncbi.nlm.nih.gov/9143069/.

McDonald, J. H., trans. *Tao Te Ching.* Updated December 6, 2007. http://www.wright-house.com/religions/taoism/tao-te-ching.html.

McGill University Office of Religious and Spiritual Life. *The MORSL Guide to Faith-Based Meditation.* Montreal: McGill University, 2020. https://www.mcgill.ca/morsl/files/morsl/morsl_meditation_guide_may_5_2020.pdf.

Monier-Williams, M. *A Sanskrit-English Dictionary: Etymologically and Philologically Arranged with Special Reference to Cognate Indo-European Languages.* Oxford: Clarendon Press, 1899. Updated May 31, 2022. https://www.wisdomlib.org/definition/dhri.

Mount Madonna School Values in World Thought. "George Lucas: Project Happiness Interview." YouTube, July 19, 2016. Video. https://www.youtube.com/watch?v=2TdGd0MlmvI&t=1014s.

Mourning Dove. *Mourning Dove: A Salishan Autobiography.* Edited by Jay Miller. Lincoln: University of Nebraska Press, 1990.

Mufti, Kamil. "Meaning of Life in Islam." *Arab News,* updated January 22, 2016. https://www.arabnews.com/islam-perspective/news/868496.

Müller, F. Max, trans. *Dhammapada, a Collection of Verses; Being One of the Canonical Books of the Buddhists.* Project Gutenberg, 1999. https://www.gutenberg.org/ebooks/2017.

Murthy, K. Krishna. "Dharma—Its Etymology." *Tibet Journal* 21, no. 1 (Spring1996): 84–87.

Nader, Tony. *Human Physiology: Expression of Veda and the Vedic Literature*. Fairfield, IA: Maharishi International University Press, 2015.

———. *Ramayan in Human Physiology*. Fairfield, IA: Maharishi International University Press, 2011.

Nanak. "Japji—The Morning Prayer." In *Japji: The Immortal Prayer-Chant*. Translated by Khushwant Singh. New Delhi: Abhinav Publications, 1987.

New Oxford American Dictionary. 3rd ed. New York: Oxford University Press, 2010.

Nolan, Jonathan, and Christopher Nolan. "*The Dark Knight*: 2008 Film." Script Slug. Accessed February 22, 2024. https://www.scriptslug.com/script/the-dark -knight-2008.

The Numbers. "Movie Franchises." Accessed February 22, 2024. https://www.the -numbers.com/movies/franchises.

OpenStax. "15.2 World Religions." Accessed February 22, 2024. https://openstax .org/books/introduction-sociology-2e/pages/15-2-world-religions.

Paramahansa Yogananda. *Sayings of Paramahansa Yogananda*. Los Angeles: Self-Realization Fellowship, 1986.

Paterson, Debs, dir. *The Skywalker Legacy: The Making of* Star Wars: Episode IX—The Rise of Skywalker *(2019)*. San Francisco: Lucasfilm, 2020. DVD.

PBS. "Basics of Buddhism." Accessed February 22, 2024. https://www.pbs.org/ edens/thailand/buddhism.htm.

Pearson, Craig. *The Supreme Awakening: Experiences of Enlightenment Throughout Time—and How You Can Cultivate Them*. Fairfield, IA: Maharishi International University Press, 2016.

Penn, William. "Prayer." In Michael Smathers, *Let Them Be Not Forgotten: Eulogies Written in a Country Churchyard, 1974–2015*, 383. N.p.: Xlibris, 2016.

Physics Classroom. "Newton's Third Law." Accessed February 22, 2024. https:// www.physicsclassroom.com/class/newtlaws/Lesson-4/Newton-s-Third-Law.

Player, Gary. Foreword to Ernie Els, *How to Build a Classic Golf Swing*, 6. New York: Harper Perennial, 1999.

Pranic Healers. "Noble Eightfold Path." Accessed February 22, 2024. https://www .thepranichealers.com/eightfold-path.

Quote Investigator. "You Are Not a Human Being Having a Spiritual Experience. You Are a Spiritual Being Having a Human Experience." June 20, 2019. https:// quoteinvestigator.com/2019/06/20/spiritual/.

Quranic Arabic Corpus. "Verse (3:191)—English Translation." Accessed February 22, 2024. https://corpus.quran.com/translation.jsp?chapter=3&verse=191.

Radhakrishnan, S., trans. *The Bhagavadgita*. New York: HarperCollins, 2010.

Ram Dass. *Be Here Now*. New York: HarperCollins, 2010. Kindle.

———. "Being Love." Accessed February 22, 2024. https://www.ramdass.org/ being-love/.

Red Cloud. "I Represent the Whole Sioux Nation, and They Will Be Bound by What I Say." In *Indian Oratory: Famous Speeches by Noted Indian Chieftains*, compiled by W. C. Vanderwerth, 188–92. Norman: University of Oklahoma Press, 1971.

Rinzler, J. W. *The Making of* Star Wars. New York: Ballantine Books, 2007.

Roth, Veronica. *Divergent*. London: HarperCollins, 2012.

Rumi, Jalal al-Din. "We Can See the Truth in Your Eyes." In *Rumi: In the Arms of the Beloved*, translated by Jonathan Star, 3–5. New York: Penguin, 2008.

Sadhguru. "The Eternal Outlaw." In Sadhguru and Arundhathi Subramaniam, *Adiyogi: The Source of Yoga*, 35–42. New York: HarperCollins, 2017.

———. *Of Mystics and Mistakes*. Ahmedabad: Jaico Publishing House, 2012.

Samye Institute. "Four Truths of the Noble Ones." Accessed February 22, 2024. https://www.samyeinstitute.org/wiki/four-truths-of-the-noble-ones/.

Schimmel, Annemarie. "Islam: Tales and Legends Concerning Religious Figures." Encyclopedia Britannica. Accessed February 22, 2024. https://www.britannica.com/topic/Islam/Tales-and-legends-concerning-religious-figures.

Sekaquaptewa, Emory, Kenneth C. Hill, and Dorothy K. Washburn. *Hopi Katsina Songs*. Lincoln: University of Nebraska Press, 2015.

Shankar, Ravi. "Chapter 11: The Six Distortions of Love." In *Wisdom for the New Millennium*, 92–99. Mumbai, India: Aslan Reads, 2019.

Singh, Mohinder. "Sikhism: Transcendental and Interfaith Message." In *World Religions: Diversity, Not Dissension*, edited by Anindita N. Balslev, 33–42. New Delhi: SAGE India, 2014.

Spohn, William C. *Go and Do Likewise: Jesus and Ethics*. New York: Continuum, 1999.

Srivastava, Om Prie. Introduction to *Bhagavad Gita: The Art and Science of Management for the 21st Century*, 1–11. India: Zorba Books, 2018.

Star Wars Comparison. "Original Emperor's Message—*The Empire Strikes Back* (1980)." YouTube, October 10, 2016. Video. https://www.youtube.com/watch?v=tzUg74pcvc8.

Star Wars Fanpedia. "List of References to *Star Wars* in Movies." Accessed February 22, 2024. https://starwarsfans.fandom.com/wiki/List_of_references_to_Star_Wars_in_movies.

———. "List of References to *Star Wars* in Television." Accessed February 22, 2024. https://starwarsfans.fandom.com/wiki/List_of_references_to_Star_Wars_in_television.

Swatman, Rachel. "1977: Highest-Grossing Sci-Fi Series at the Box Office." Guinness World Records, August 19, 2015. https://www.guinnessworldrecords.com/news/60at60/2015/8/1977-highest-grossing-sci-fi-series-at-the-box-office-392957/.

Tamura, Leslie. "The Key to David Lynch's Happy Life." *Washington Post*, June 20, 2011. https://www.washingtonpost.com/national/the-key-to-david-lynchs-happy-life/2011/06/10/AGmR8NdH_story.html.

Taylor, Chris. *How* Star Wars *Conquered the Universe: The Past, Present, and Future of a Multibillion Dollar Franchise.* New York: Basic Books, 2014.

Titelman, Carol, ed. *The Art of* Star Wars. New York: Ballantine Books, 1979.

Titmuss, Christopher. "Four Truths of the Noble Ones." Accessed February 22, 2024. https://www.christophertitmuss.net/four-truths-of-the-noble-ones.

Travis, Frederick. "Transcendental Experiences during Meditation Practice." *Annals of the New York Academy of Sciences* 1307 (January 2014): 1–8. https://pubmed.ncbi .nlm.nih.gov/24673148/.

Travis, Frederick, Alarik Arenander, and David DuBois. "Psychological and Physiological Characteristics of a Proposed Object-Referral/Self-Referral Continuum of Self-Awareness." *Consciousness and Cognition* 13, no. 2 (April 2004): 401–20. https://pubmed.ncbi.nlm.nih.gov/15134768/.

Travis, Frederick, and David Orme-Johnson. "Field Model of Consciousness: EEG Coherence Changes as Indicators of Field Effects." *International Journal of Neuroscience* 49, nos. 3–4 (December 1989): 203–11. https://pubmed.ncbi.nlm .nih.gov/2700478/.

Travis, Frederick, and Craig Pearson. "Pure Consciousness: Distinct Phenomenological and Physiological Correlates of 'Consciousness Itself.'" *International Journal of Neuroscience* 100, nos. 1–4 (February 2000): 77–89. https://pubmed.ncbi.nlm.nih .gov/10512549/.

Travis, Frederick, and Jonathan Shear. "Focused Attention, Open Monitoring and Automatic Self-Transcending: Categories to Organize Meditations from Vedic, Buddhist and Chinese Traditions." *Consciousness and Cognition* 19, no. 4 (February 2010): 1110–18. https://pubmed.ncbi.nlm.nih.gov/20167507/.

Travis, Frederick, Joe Tecce, Alarik Arenander, R. Keith Wallace. "Patterns of EEG Coherence, Power, and Contingent Negative Variation Characterize the Integration of Transcendental and Waking States." *Biological Psychology* 61, no. 3 (November 2002): 293–319. https://pubmed.ncbi.nlm.nih.gov/12406612/.

Windham, Ryder. Star Wars Episode I: The Phantom Menace *Movie Scrapbook.* New York: Random House, 1999.

Winnemucca, Sarah. "The Pah-Utes." *Californian* 6, no. 33 (September 1882): 252–56. Reprinted in *The Sagebrush Anthology: Literature from the Silver Age of the Old West*, edited by Lawrence I. Berkove, 328–35. Columbia: University of Missouri Press, 2006.

Wookieepedia. "Force Dyad." Accessed February 22, 2024. https://starwars.fandom .com/wiki/Force_dyad.

———. "Oneness." Accessed February 22, 2024. https://starwars.fandom.com/wiki /Oneness.

Yanek, Dawn. "May the 4th Be with You: All about the *Star Wars* Holiday." *Reader's Digest*, April 29, 2022. https://www.rd.com/article/may-the-fourth-star-wars -holiday/.

Yellow Lark, trans. "Prayer for Appreciation." In James P. Moore Jr., *The Treasury of American Prayer*, 84. New York: Doubleday, 2008.

"'You've Got to Find What You Love,' Jobs Says." *Stanford News*, June 12, 2005. https://news.stanford.edu/2005/06/12/youve-got-find-love-jobs-says/.

Zhuangzi. *The Complete Works of Zhuangzi*. Translated by Burton Watson. New York: Columbia University Press, 2013.

Zona, Guy, comp. *The Soul Would Have No Rainbow If the Eyes Had No Tears—and Other Native American Proverbs*. New York: Touchstone, 1994.

INDEX

ABOUT THE AUTHOR

Krista Noble has a PhD and an MA in Vedic (ancient Indian) studies from Maharishi International University (MIU). She is an expert on the Consciousness-Based Vedic paradigm and received MIU's Veda Vyasa Award. She is also a lifetime member of the World Association for Vedic Studies.

Dr. Noble is a professor of Vedic studies at Maharishi International University and the Holmes Institute. In addition, she has taught at the University of Philosophical Research.

Dr. Noble has published works in the proceedings of the 2018 World Association for Vedic Studies conference and the 2022 international Science of Consciousness conference. Her writings have appeared in national magazines and literary journals, including *New Age Journal*, *The Penwood Review*, *WestWard Quarterly*, *The Storyteller*, *Ceremony*, *The Acorn*, *Advocate: P.K.A.'s Publication*, *Nature Friend*, *Grit*, *Farm & Ranch Living*, *Countryside*, and *Home Educator's Family Times*.

Dr. Noble is a seasoned and dynamic public speaker, having presented at the World Association for Vedic Studies conference, the Science and Scientist conference, the Science of Consciousness conference, Loyola Marymount University, Stetson University, and other, less traditional outlets (Nerd Nite, podcasts, meditation centers, and more).

To learn more about Dr. Noble's professional activities, visit her website at https://kristanoble.com.

www.ingramcontent.com/pod-product-compliance
Lightning Source LLC
Chambersburg PA
CBHW030307100426
42812CB00002B/602